THE LORD IS MY SHEPHERD

Also by William Barclay in this series

The Apostles' Creed
At the Last Trumpet
Discovering Jesus
Good Tidings of Great Joy
Great Themes of the New Testament
Growing in Christian Faith
Letters to the Seven Churches
The Lord's Prayer
The Lord's Supper
Many Witnesses, One Lord
The New Testament
New Testament Words
The Parables of Jesus
The Promise of the Spirit
The Ten Commandments
We Have Seen the Lord!

The Lord is My Shepherd

William Barclay

Westminster John Knox Press
LOUISVILLE
LONDON • LEIDEN

Published in the U.S.A. in 2001 by
Westminster John Knox Press
Louisville, Kentucky

Original edition published in English under the title
The Lord is My Shepherd by John Hunt Publishing Ltd.,
46a West Street, New Alresford, Hants, UK.

PRINTED IN HONG KONG/CHINA

01 02 03 04 05 06 07 08 09 10 — 10 9 8 7 6 5 4 3 2 1

Library of Congress Cataloging-in-Publication Data
Barclay, William, 1907-1978.
    The Lord is my shepherd / William Barclay.
        p. cm.
    Originally published: Philadelphia : Westminister Press, c1980.
    ISBN 0-664-22384-2 (alk. paper)
    1. Bible. O.T. Psalms--Criticism, interpretation, etc. I. Bible. O.T.
Psalms. English. Seclections. 2001. II. Title.

BS1430.52.B37 2001
223'.206--dc21

                                                    00-065477

Contents

A Man and His God

by Allan Galloway

The only memorial that William Barclay would have wished for himself is that written on the hearts of people who remember him with affection and gratitude. Such a memorial he certainly has. There may have been biblical scholars of greater distinction; but none has ever exercised such vast popular appeal as he did. In every continent of the English-speaking world he is known and remembered by a grateful public.

To that public he gave himself with such energy and single-minded devotion that it consumed his whole life. He earned the respect and affection which such vast numbers of us feel towards him. If not for his sake, at least for ours, we need some concrete symbol in which our gratitude can find a point of focus and expression.

But to construct a memorial to the Reverend Professor William Barclay, DD – to do it decently and in a manner proper to the man – is not easy. He detested and despised empty formality. Any of the conventional forms of memorial would be quite inappropriate.

But what could be more appropriate than to have the last living words of the man himself published as a memorial to be cherished with the memory of him.

This is a volume in which for the last time we hear his distinctive voice, savor the direct simplicity of his style, the illumination of simple things in his thought, enjoy the warmth of his humanity and share the sincerity of his piety.

The phrase 'vintage Barclay' has been used of what he has

1

written here. This is a felicitous description of the work of his last months. His health was failing. The prodigious pace of his work had slowed to a gentle meandering. Behind him lay all the richness of a full life. The phrase 'vintage Barclay' is very appropriate.

But in another sense this is 'new-growth Barclay'. Willie, as he allowed both friends and strangers to call him, had just about written himself out on the New Testament. In his last years he began to turn his mind towards the Old Testament. As ever he brought to it an approach which was fresh and lively.

In a sense, what William Barclay did for the New Testament was to rescue it from the experts. He renewed its availability to the plain man. This was done without any sacrifice of his own scholarship or scholarly standards. His interpretations may often have amounted to over-simplification. But they were always born of elaborate erudition. Had he lived longer he would have brought the same kind of scholarship, tempered by the same kind of common-sense simplicity, to the Old Testament.

As it is we have only a tiny sample of what he might have done. He had begun with the Psalms. His treatment even of them is woefully incomplete. The very scarcity of Barclay on the Old Testament makes this a rare vintage indeed. For those who enjoy and have profited from his biblical expositions this will be something unique and precious.

His spiritual approach to the Old Testament was that of a Christian. It is a source of nourishment for the Christian life. Long before he turned directly to this primarily Jewish book his lively interpretations of the New Testament owed much to his appreciation of the role played by the Old in the life and thought of the early Church. He never allowed himself to forget that Jesus was and remained a Jew, however original and deviant his interpretations and development of the faith of Abraham may have been.

The title proposed for this book was *The Lord is my Shepherd*. As it turned out, William Barclay never did get to the point of setting his thoughts on the 23rd Psalm down on paper. More's the pity! It would have been good to have heard him on the subject. Nevertheless the title still seems appropriate. It sums up the spirit of the man as well as the heart of his theme.

I have never known anyone so universally and unanimously liked as William Barclay. The millions who knew him only through his writing felt the attraction of his personality almost as keenly as those of us who were his colleagues and acquaintances. To share memories of such a man is sheer delight even though tempered by sadness at his death.

Fame came relatively late to William Barclay. He was born in Wick in 1907. His father was a bank manager. In 1912 the family moved to Motherwell and William attended Dalziel High School. In these early days, though he performed creditably as a scholar and was awarded the prize in Classics, he distinguished himself even more as an athlete. He was Scottish Schoolboy Hundred Yards Champion.

He became an undergraduate in the University of Glasgow in 1925. Four years later he graduated, a distinguished First in Classics. He then became a student in the Faculty of Divinity. In those days all the Scottish Divinity Faculties required an Arts Degree as a condition of admission to study for the Degree of Bachelor of Divinity. This was a wholesome custom which has been abandoned only with regret in these days of educational impoverishment. His studies in the Faculty of Arts laid the foundation of that broad and cultivated humanity which so winsomely informed the spirit of his theology. In his autobiographical book *Testament of Faith* he speaks with great reverence of his University teachers. It was not so much for their erudition as for their wisdom and the quality of their personalities that he remembered and revered them. This was especially true of his Professor of Moral Philosophy – A. A. Bowman. In these reminiscences William Barclay made it clear that he received as much spiritual nourishment from his studies in the Faculty of Arts as he did in the Faculty of Divinity.

Another wholesome custom of those early days was that every man who was one day to teach in a Scottish Faculty of Divinity was expected to do a tour of duty ministering to a parish of the Church before he mounted the rostrum to tell young ordinands what it was all about. William Barclay received such a grounding in the realities of God's way with men as minister of Trinity Church, Renfrew, from 1933 to 1946. It was there that he learned to unite his scholarly interests with pastoral concern in a way which formed the peculiar genius of all his theological writing. His pastoral gifts and concerns were never, as is sadly so often the case, isolated from his biblical and theological scholarship. It was in that parish that he learned that faithful and meticulous study of the word of God and its application to the souls of men and women from a single continuum. For him the meaning of a biblical passage had not been expounded until its pastoral significance had been elicited. This made him very impatient of every kind of theological or ecclesiastical claptrap.

He always maintained that it was in this period of parish ministry that his main theological stance and style were formed. He attributed this largely to the people of his parish. He insisted that he learned far more from them than they did from him. No matter what erudition we bring to the study of Scripture it is the people who provide the context for its interpretation.

If I were to attempt to characterize the remarkable theological style which emerged from this substantial period of pastoral apprenticeship, I should say that it was that of a man who believed that God is not only all wise but also has common sense, that he not only loves us eternally but likes us as well.

Though he eventually became a figure of such profound

pastoral significance to millions of people, he never consciously posed as such or adopted such a role. He tended rather to see himself in the role of God's jester – as the fool whom only the grace of God rescued from the very brink of folly. It was perhaps for this reason that he loved to tell stories against himself. This is illustrated in a story he used to tell about the days of his pastoral experience. He was visiting a woman who was suffering from severe depression. Dramatically she announced her intention of ending it all by drowning herself in the river. But the young William Barclay, who suffered even then from the hearing defect which became severe in later life, did not quite hear what she had said. Being unwilling to ask the woman to repeat something which had been said with such obvious distress, he thought it best to give her encouragement by saying, 'An excellent idea! I couldn't suggest anything better myself.' What could the poor woman do but laugh? Not only did she not commit suicide but, he claimed, her cure began from that day. He had been the instrument but not the agent. He continued to feel like that about his role even when he became the spiritual mentor of millions.

When he returned to Glasgow University in 1947 as a lecturer in New Testament his special qualities as a teacher immediately became apparent. His lectures had the same remarkable quality as his books. He tended to stress the essential simplicities of the biblical message and to make light of its inessential complexities. A somewhat daring and indeed reckless hermeneutical principle underlies this policy. It rested on the assumption that the traditionally acclaimed simplicity of God is not merely a metaphysical principle but a plain fact of his dealing with men. The heart of this fact was his taking simple human nature upon himself.

But this simplicity, which William Barclay consciously strove to emulate, is very different from mere naïveté. The simplicity of Jesus was one of the most disconcerting features of his person. One of the best authenticated elements in the Gospel story is that the scholars and rabbis of Jesus' day tried again and again to draw him into their complex debates about the interpretation of the law and the Prophets. He always countered this move with a retort so penetrating and questioning in its simplicity that his questioners were driven into thoughtful and disconcerted silence. It was this example which encouraged William Barclay in his determination never to allow the complexities of contemporary scholarship to obscure the heart of the matter. The fact that his unquestioned erudition was tempered and matured by this principle made him one of the most influential teachers of our age. His appointment to the Chair of New Testament in the University of Glasgow when it fell vacant in 1963 gave universal satisfaction.

His industry in those days was quite astonishing and remained so right up to those latter years in which illness diminished his energy. His retiring room in the Faculty building was next to mine. On the very rare occasions on which I was in my room before 7 a.m. his typewriter was already clicking away. On the even rarer occasions when I was still in the department at midnight the same typewriter was still to be heard. The sheer quantity of his output of some sixty books, coupled with their multi-millions sales figures, beggar all superlatives. His *Daily Study Bible* series, the commentaries in which were originally written to assist and inform lay devotional reading of the Bible, are widely used as aids to study in theological seminaries throughout the English-speaking world. These and his *Plain Man's Guide* series bridged the gap between technical New Testament scholarship and lay enquiry in a way which no other writer has ever achieved.

To this prodigious output he added, in the years of his maturity, when lesser men would have been slowing down, a resounding success as a television and radio lecturer. His popularity rating on television was almost as remarkable as his publication statistics. His expressive, rugged face, his deep, gravelly voice and his characteristic gestures became familiar to the nation.

I recall an incident during this period of the ascendancy of his public image which well illustrates the extent of his popularity. I was driving through a beautiful village on the Firth of Clyde one Sunday about the hour of Evening Service. I thought to share in evening worship at the village church. The notice-board confirmed that there was indeed a diet of worship at 6.30 p.m. I found the church deserted. I finally found a caretaker who told me that the evening service had been cancelled because William Barclay was lecturing on television! What higher compliment could be paid to a man of God by the people of God?

He remained unspoiled by fame. When he spoke of himself it was usually to tell stories at his own expense. I still cherish his own account of how he was sitting alone in the lounge of a hotel when a stranger came up to him and said, with the excessive heartiness of one who has perhaps imbibed a little too freely, 'I know your face; but I cannot remember your name.' Then light seemed to dawn and the stranger exclaimed, 'I've got it, you're one of those Sunday night comics on the television!' There was perhaps just a grain of truth in this identification. He did entertain as he instructed. He had a ready wit and an endless store of entertaining instances. His lectures were frequently punctuated by the laughter of his students.

But it is for his writing that he will be remembered by most. He held a unique position among New Testament scholars. In an age when biblical criticism became almost synonymous with historical scepticism he remained stoutly convinced that we could not only, with reasonable confidence, give an adequately full account of the events of Jesus' ministry; but he also held that, because of the genius of the Gospels and the peculiar power of their inspiration, we can know him better and more intimately than we know anyone else.

Another New Testament scholar once made the rather snide remark, 'William Barclay – isn't that the fellow who tells you what Jesus had for breakfast?'. To that remark one might well reply, 'Yes indeed! if you can establish the time of year and the locality, he probably could tell you what Jesus had for breakfast'. He was a man of enormous erudition about the biblical and classical world. He had done such meticulous research into the details of everyday life in the world in which Jesus lived that he could fill in the picture of events merely hinted at in the New Testament narrative. Again and again this was what enabled him to make the story live and to show its human relevance.

His erudition, which he never paraded, was of gargantuan proportions. He had a virtually photographic memory throughout most of his life. Without reference to notes he could supply astonishingly detailed information. He could, when occasion demanded it, quote with accuracy and relevance from an astonishing range of both ancient and modern literature. He could often supply even the exact reference from memory. This was one of the gifts which enabled him to write his books with such facility and such fluency.

Had he used his energies in accordance with more traditional styles of biblical scholarship he could have left behind him some highly specialized monographs – especially on the social and cultural background of the New Testament. But he was a popularizer and reveled in the fact. He used to boast with a characteristically mischievous glee that he had never had an original idea in his life, that he merely interpreted the ideas of others. This may have been a decently modest statement, but it is quite untrue. A great many of his ideas on both the translation and the interpretation of the New Testament were of intriguing, sometimes even startling novelty. He was a popularizer only in the sense that he did not write for other professional scholars but for his students and the public. Being quite uniquely gifted to do so, he chose throughout his life to expose the fruits rather than the roots of his learning.

It is always difficult to analyse the secret virtue which makes so astonishingly popular and successful a writer. I venture to think, however, that Professor Barclay's remarkable success as a writer was due, in the first instance, neither to his literary facility nor his great intellectual powers, which are both beyond question, but to the openness, simplicity and directness of his personality. No artifice or calculated effect ever came between him and his audience whether in simple conversation, in the classroom, before a television camera, or addressing the millions of his readers. He had the capacity to make himself unaffectedly present to his audience no matter what the medium of communication. The after-image of his presence remains so vividly in the memory that it is difficult to realize that he is no longer with us. He was loved by his public as much as he was followed and admired.

He reciprocated this affection in a way that should perhaps be better known. His extensive popularity as a writer and broadcaster brought an ever increasing body of mail to his desk. Every enquiry, every argument, every problem received a courteous and painstaking reply. Even foolish letters which other busy men might have thrown in the wastepaper basket received this treatment. Caring for the truth of God and caring for people were for him inseparable.

His true memorial, however, is the legend which he has left behind him. Few men become a legend in their own lifetime. He did. He really was a man larger than life and twice as natural.

BARCLAY ON THE PSALMS

The Psalms of the Old Testament have nourished the spirit of the Jewish people for two to three thousand years. They have sustained the devotion of the Christian Church since its foundation. Their true context is not 'once-upon-a-time-long-ago', but the whole history in which they have been an active ingredient.

A faithful exposition of the Psalms must therefore never become an exercise in literary archaeology. It must exhibit their power of contemporaneity through the ages. It should illuminate their role in the immediate nurture of the human spirit.

This timeless vitality of the Psalms is prominent in William Barclay's treatment of them. For example he opens his treatment of the first Psalm by recollecting comparable echoes of its main theme. He refers to the Book of Proverbs. Then he jumps forward to St Matthew's Gospel. He moves forward again to *The Teaching of the Twelve Apostles* and *The Letter of Barnabas*, both works from the beginning of the Christian era. Back again to *The Secrets of Enoch* – a late Jewish apocalypse written perhaps a hundred years before Christ. Then forward to John Oxenham, then back again to another Psalm, and so on. He ranges back and forwards through the millennia. It is as though, before the splendor of the Psalms, all the ages are reduced to the proportions of the day as in the sight of God.

These are not so much commentaries as meditations upon the Psalms. He wanders slowly through each of the five Psalms he treats, allowing the light of each verse, each idea, to fall upon his mind and reveal what it may. Each verse and each theme generates its own association of ideas. In a sense you could say that these commentaries are just the meanderings of an old man. Yes indeed; but what a remarkable old man! I have already spoken of his gift of almost perfect recall for nearly everything that he had ever read. This gives a richness to his meditation which – at least for those few Psalms – we are able to share.

He speaks about the Jewish understanding of meditation upon the law (p. 32): 'The idea . . . was for a man to so soak himself in the law that it pervaded his whole being.' In the same way William Barclay invites us to learn to so soak ourselves in the devotion of the Psalms that it pervades our whole being and it plays its light over the whole content of our minds.

It is in the same meditative way that this book itself should be read. For anyone who thinks he does not know how to meditate then here's how! William Barclay leads us by the hand through meditation after meditation. If we work our way slowly and thoughtfully through these meditations on five Psalms – possibly following the Jewish practice which involved reading slowly and quietly aloud – we may by the end have got the hang of it, so that we can go on to practise it for ourselves.

A good example of his style of pious meditation informed by scholarship is his treatment of the first verse of Psalm 8. The Hebrew is obscure and translation of this verse has for long been a matter of puzzlement and controversy. William Barclay acknowledges four main possibilities of interpretation. But instead of diverting attention to the technical problems of deciding between these possibilities, he takes up all four of them as live options and weaves them into a delicate and suggestive meditation upon the praise and honor which accrue to God from every creature – from angels to little children and even from his enemies.

This meditative and devotional interpretation of the Psalms centers upon two main themes – creation and law. It is like old times to have these recognized as the two main *foci* of Old Testament theology. The recent trend has been to treat covenant and prophetic promise as the keys to its meaning. But this trend is largely the product of a tendency to treat the Old Testament merely as a preparation for the Gospel.

No one could have gone further than William Barclay did in exalting redemption above creation, grace above law. But in his treatment of the Old Testament he is content to let it remain what it essentially is – a Jewish Book. Certainly as a Christian and a New Testament scholar, he finds in Jesus Christ a fulfilment both of what the Old Testament declared and of what it demanded. For example his treatment of Psalm 8 ends with the contention that 'it is concerned with the creation of man and not his fall, for it is telling of God's purpose for man and the destiny God gave him. That is why the Christian Church annexed this Psalm, especially the writer to the Hebrews (Hebrews 2.5-9). What man failed to do the great Son of Man can do. In Jesus Christ man reaches his ideal and his destiny; in Jesus Christ man is what God meant him to be, and therefore his is the final Lordship and dominion. What man cannot do for himself Jesus Christ does for him' (Psalm 8).

Thus, without relinquishing anything of the Christian claim to find support, inspiration and instruction in the Old Testament, he none the less allows it to keep its own Jewish identity. But such is the open nature of truly Jewish piety that this does not restrict its relevance. Rather it discloses the universality of its appeal. The doctrine of creation declares that every creature is the creature of God. The promulgation of the law declares that every creature is under the care of God.

William Barclay was always deeply conscious of the way in which the whole of creation and every creature within it bears the stamp of its maker. This is its glory and its meaning. He is very much at home with his text when the theme is like that of the opening verses of Psalm 19.1, 2

> The heavens are telling the glory of God;
> and the firmament proclaims his handiwork.

> Day to day pours forth speech,
>> and night to night declares knowledge.

This theme, so prevalent in the Psalms and so deeply grounded in Jewish tradition, chimed in harmoniously with a natural inclination of William Barclay's mind and personality. He cherished all creatures in a bonhomous enjoyment of them. He retained throughout his life that sense of astonished wonder at the marvelous complexity, the vast proportions and the breathtaking beauty of the world which is normally the privilege only of the child. In *Testament of Faith* he acknowledged the importance of this perception of the world as a ground of his faith. He there attempted (in one of his questionable excursions into the realms of philosophy) to give this systematic expression by reviving Paley's much criticized argument that, just as we might infer the existence of a watchmaker from a watch, so we may infer the existence of God from the order of the universe. But what William Barclay is concerned with here is not really a philosophical inference. It is rather an openness to the world and to the self-disclosure of God in the world which is prior to all philosophical reflection. It is a perception which must remain ultimately inarticulate. It can be shared only in communion. The commentator can only point to it. He cannot express it.

> There is no speech, nor are there words;
>> their voice is not heard;
> yet their voice goes out through all the earth,
>> and their words to the end of the world
>
> (Psalm 19.3)

Of this he says 'the point is not that words and speech have gone out to the end of the earth but that, although in nature there are no words, there is an eloquent silence in which God makes himself known'. (Psalm 19). It is something shared and communicated in the communion of Christ.

This exaltation of the voice of nature in the Psalms was clearly something of great importance to William Barclay. It was not for him a thing of romantic sentimentality but of down-to-earth, everyday reality. For him there was no tension between natural and revealed religion. They formed an unbroken continuum.

Like many I have often pondered upon the remarkable success of William Barclay as a popular religious writer. One ingredient in the secret of his success was this unusual sensitivity to the intimations of God in the everyday commonalities of the created order. It was of this too that the parables of Jesus spoke. This was the theological foundation on which he became the unrivalled interpreter of Scripture for 'the plain man'.

The other aspect of the Psalms which grasped his attention was their exaltation of the law of God. This too was something which found a ready response in him. Just as he found no tension between natural and revealed religion, so he found no contradiction between the law and Grace of God. Although certainly not a legalist and among the most tolerant of men, he upheld the clarity and the absoluteness of the law of God all his life. This came to clear and emphatic expression when he gave his television lectures on Christian Ethics. They were delivered at a time when everyone was talking about the permissive society and its theological confederate 'situation ethics'. When everyone was inclined to emphasize the moral ambiguities of the human situation William Barclay took his stand very firmly on the proposition that right is right and wrong is wrong and the distinction between them is clearer than our sophistries are inclined to suggest. If we have become confused about it we should not extend our corruption to the moral law itself. To follow the invitation of the Psalmist to meditate upon the law of God and to extol its excellence is to seek to illuminate our confusion in the light of its clarity.

The intimate relation between the order of creation and the order of salvation was so clear that for him the relation between law and Gospel presented no problem. He saw them both as expressions of the love, constancy and splendid majesty of God. For the same reason he saw no tension between the natural moral sense of mankind and the revealed law of God. His minute studies of the Jewish background to the Gospels and to the life and teachings of Jesus gave him a sensitive appreciation of the spirit of Jewish piety. He knew that when the Psalmist invites us to meditate upon the law of God he is not merely suggesting that we should pay attention to the letter of the law – to a mere code of rules as such. He is inviting us to meditate upon the heart and mind of God which come to expression in his law. William Barclay found no problem in identifying this as the same mind and heart that came to concrete expression in Jesus Christ.

As we contemplate that heart and mind of God, whether in the law or in Jesus Christ, we come to know God as he is in himself. We know him intimately in a heart to heart relation. In this relation we also come to know ourselves as we really are. In this unity of the knowledge of God and Man we discover the unity of the revealed law of God with the created law of our consciences. Moral sense and piety thus find their ultimate identity.

It was this perception which enabled William Barclay to enter so easily and comfortably into the piety of the Psalms without in any way changing that familiar style of thought and writing which he had already developed in relation to the New Testament.

To open up the Psalms to plain folk so that they too can enter into them with the same easy piety – without engaging in unnatural contortions of mind and spirit – is a demanding task. It calls for the peculiar genius of a William Barclay.

In Christian tradition the Psalms have been the playthings of ecclesiastics for centuries. They have been the main adornment of liturgy. We count them out like the beads on a rosary throughout the Christian year. We sing them to strange, old-fashioned music which lends itself increasingly to caricature. Those of us who are professionally or vocationally engaged in such antics too readily forget how strange and unnatural all this appears to ordinary, everyday people who have not learned such elaborate chancel manners. This could be said of much of our liturgy; but particularly of our use for the Psalms.

I remember an occasion many years ago when I went to church in company with a young man released from a correctional institution on probation. He had never been to church in his life before. As we left the church I was anxious to know what impact the service had had upon one of such remarkable ecclesiastical innocence. He replied, 'I liked the hymns but I couldn't stand those *spasms*.' I have treasured that remark ever since. It sums up what the Psalms have become for so many people – spasms – unnatural and contorted activity. William Barclay had begun to show us how a plain man, in virtue of the common humanity which he shares with the Psalmist and the eternal magnificence of the reality which they adore, can still feel at home with the Psalms.

I imagine that it was to this end that he included a section on the obscure technical terms that we find scattered throughout the Psalms. I confess that my own instinct would have been to leave such technical considerations out of a popular meditation upon the Psalms. But William Barclay had a superior instinct in such matters which one must respect. If ordinary folk are to feel at home with the Psalms those strange words must be honestly looked at and sufficiently dealt with to prevent them from interfering with the plain sense of the Psalms. Such technical explanations are not important in themselves. Their function is simply to release the Psalms from the aura of strangeness that surrounds them. The aim is to let the Psalms be themselves and to let us be ourselves with them.

I have said of Willie Barclay that he was large as life and twice as natural. This was the attraction of the man and it is the attraction of his theology. He was always his natural self, unstrained and unaffected. This was the innermost secret of his astonishing success as a writer, teacher and preacher. No artifice, no pretension was ever allowed to come between him and those to whom he addressed himself.

To him piety was not an unnatural constraint upon human nature. For him piety was the most natural thing in the world. Piety is learning to feel at home with one's creator. This is also the route to being frankly and unashamedly at home with oneself.

This particular brand of godliness enhances but does not distort our natural humanity. It rests upon his perceptive appreciation of the continuity between the story of our creation and the story of our redemption – a unity in which our Fall is a mere interruption. It rests upon a perception of the unity of spirit between the Old and the New Testaments.

In a comment on Psalm 24, too fragmentary for publication in this text, he remarks that the Psalm was probably written to celebrate a victory. He goes on to say 'it is just possible that there is another kind of victory at the back of this. Verse 2 says that God has founded the world upon the seas and established it upon the rivers. Creation in the ancient stories was not only an act, it was a victory; a victory over the goddess of chaos, Taimat, and a victory in which chaos was brought to order.' This sense of the glorious triumph of God proceeding in unbroken continuity from the very beginning of creation of the very end of time, finally and invincibly triumphant over all sin, disorder and suffering, is the heart of Willie Barclay's theology. He found it in the trust of Jesus in his Heavenly Father. He finds it anticipated in the Psalms.

And so with the Psalmist he can love the natural world and the natural man with an uninhibited and forgiving generosity of spirit which he saw as the only proper response to the prevenient generosity of God.

Dr Barclay received of that generosity of God in full measure. He was a man of very special talents of mind and spirit. He gave in the measure in which he received. His life was a prodigious labor of writing. It was a labor of love. He died, as he would have wished, in the midst of it.

> Thou hast made the moon to mark the seasons;
>> the sun knows its time for setting.
> Thou makest darkness, and it is night,
>> when all the beasts of the forest creep forth.
> The young lions roar for their prey,
>> seeking their food from God.
> When the sun rises, they get them away
>> and lie down in their dens.
> Man goes forth to his work
>> and to his labor until the evening
>
> (Psalm 104.19-23)

Approaching The Psalms

The Book of Psalms contains the whole music of the heart of
man, swept like a harp by the hand of his Maker. In it are
gathered the lyrical burst of his tenderness, the moan of his
penitence, the pathos of his sorrow, the triumph of his victory,
the despair of his defeat, the firmness of his confidence, the
rapture of his assured hope. In it is presented the anatomy of all
parts of the human soul; in it, as Heine says, are collected
'sunrise and sunset, birth and death, promise and fulfilment –
the whole drama of humanity'.

R. E. Prothero, *The Psalms in Human Life*

There you look into the hearts of all the saints as into a beautiful
gay garden, indeed as into heaven; and in that garden you see
spring up lovely, bright, charming flowers, flowers of all sorts of
beautiful and joyous thoughts about God and his mercy. Again,
where do you find words expressing sorrow more deeply and
picturing its misery and wretchedness more tellingly than the
words that are contained in the psalms of lament? Here you
look once more into the hearts of all the saints as into death,
indeed as into hell; how dark and gloomy it is there, because of
the grievous spectacle of the wrath of God which has to be faced
in so many ways! Again, wherever they speak of fear or hope,
they use such words that no painter could portray either fear or
hope with equal force and no Cicero or orator could fashion
them in like manner. And the very best thing is that they speak
such words about God and to God . . .

This explains, moreover, why the Psalter is the favorite book
of all the saints, and why each one of them, whatever his

circumstances may be, finds in it psalms and words which are appropriate to the circumstances in which he finds himself and meet his needs as adequately as if they were composed exclusively for his sake, and in such a way that he himself could not improve on them nor could find or desire any better psalms or words . . .

To sum up: if you want to see the holy Christian Church painted in glowing colours and in a form which is really alive, and if you want this to be done in a miniature, you must get hold of the Psalter, and there you will have in your possession a fine, clear, pure mirror which will show you what Christianity really is; yea, you will find yourself in it and the true *gnothi seauton* (know thyself), and God himself and all his creatures, too.

Luther's Preface to the German Psalter 1528

No single book of Scripture, not even of the New Testament, has, perhaps, ever taken such hold on the *heart* of Christendom. None, if we may dare judge, unless it be the Gospels, has had so large an influence in moulding the affections, sustaining the hopes, purifying the faith of believers. With its words, rather than with their own, they have come before God. In these they have uttered their desires, their fears, their confessions, their aspirations, their sorrows, their joys, their thanksgivings. By these their devotion has been kindled and their hearts comforted. The Psalter has been, in the truest sense, the Prayer Book of Jews and Christians.

Bishop Perowne, *The Book of Psalms*

Wherever you turn the laborer at the plough sings Alleluia: the toiling reaper beguiles his work with Psalms: the vine-dresser as he prunes the vine with his curved pruning-hook sings something of David's. There are the songs of this province:

these, to use the common phrase, are its love ditties: these the shepherd whistles: these are the laborer's implements.

Jerome writing from Bethlehem, *Letter 46*

To his study of the Psalms . . . the student must bring, not the detached spirit of an anatomist, or of a visitor from another planet, but the sympathy born of consciousness that the essentials of religion are permanent, and that modern thoughts and beliefs may often be folded up in ancient gems.

T. K. Cheyne, *The Book of Psalms*

Psalm 1

A GOOD MAN

Blessed is the man
　　who walks not in the counsel of the wicked,
nor stands in the way of sinners,
　　nor sits in the seat of scoffers;
2　but his delight is in the law of the LORD,
　　and on his law he meditates day and night.
3　He is like a tree
　　planted by streams of water,
that yields its fruit in its season,
　　and its leaf does not wither.
In all that he does, he prospers.

4　The wicked are not so,
　　but are like chaff which the wind drives away.
5　Therefore the wicked will not stand in the judgment,
　　nor sinners in the congregation of the righteous;
6　for the LORD knows the way of the righteous,
　　but the way of the wicked will perish.

Verse 1　WHAT THE GOOD MAN AVOIDS

The first Psalm is a summary of the very essence of Psalms, because it is a plea for the two things on which all religion depends – obedience to the word of God and trust in his providence.

It might be entitled 'Religion in Black and White'. It sets out the difference between the good and the bad man, both in regard to character and to destiny, in terms of absolute contrast. It sets out the situation which the Book of Proverbs so often describes:

> So you will walk in the way of good men
>   and keep to the paths of the righteous.
> For the upright will inhabit the land,
>   and men of integrity will remain in it;
> but the wicked will be cut off from the land,
>   and the treacherous will be rooted out of it
>
>   (Proverbs 2.20-22)

The Psalm does this by painting the picture of The Two Ways. Weiser says that this first Psalm stands at the beginning of the book like a signpost, giving clear guidance regarding the way in which all God-fearing people shall conduct their lives.

The picture of The Two Ways became basic to the expression of religion. Jesus used it:

> Enter by the narrow gate; for the gate is wide and the way is easy, that leads to destruction, and those who enter by it are many. For the gate is narrow and the way is hard, that leads to life, and those who find it are few
>
>   (Matthew 7.13, 14)

The Teaching of the Twelve Apostles, written about AD 100, begins:

> There are two ways, one of Life and one of Death, and there is a great difference between the two ways.

Another very early Christian book, *The Letter of Barnabas*, has the same picture:

There are two ways of teaching and power, one of Light and one of Darkness. And there is a great difference between the two ways. For over the one are set light-bringing angels of God, but over the other angels of Satan. And the one is Lord from eternity to eternity, and the other is the ruler of the present time of iniquity

(Letter of Barnabas 18).

The Jewish book, *The Secrets of Enoch*, takes the picture of the two ways right back to the beginning:

God places the two ways before Adam and says: I gave him his will, and I showed him the two ways, the light and the darkness. And I said to him: This is the good and this is the evil, so that I might know whether he has love for me or hate.

John Oxenham put it into poetry:

To every man there openeth
A way and ways and a way,
And the high soul takes the high way,
And the low soul gropes the low,
And in between on the misty flats
The rest drift to and fro.
But to every man there openeth
A high way and a low,
And every man decideth
The way his soul shall go.

It was true in the days of the Psalmist and it is still true that all life concentrates on man at the crossroads.

The Psalm begins with an exclamation of rapture rather than a plain statement:

Blessed is the man
who walks not in the counsel of the wicked.

This is a way of speaking which the Book of Psalms uses fairly often. It knows of the bliss of the man who takes refuge in God (Psalm 34.8); the bliss of the man who reverently fears the Lord (Psalm 112.1); the bliss of the man whose children are many (Psalm 127.5). God's man is a happy man.

The Psalm opens with a description of the things which the good man does not do.

i. He does not walk in the counsel of the wicked; that is to say, the good man does not allow himself to be guided by the advice of evil men. II Chronicles 22.3-5 gives us an illustration of this way of speaking. It tells us of Ahaziah:

> He also walked in the ways of the house of Ahab, for his mother was his counselor in doing wickedly. He did what was evil in the sight of the Lord, as the house of Ahab had done; for, after the death of his father they were his counselors, to his undoing. He even followed their counsel and went with Jehoram the son of Ahab king of Israel to make war against Hazael king of Syria at Ramoth-Gilead.

Micah accuses his countrymen:

> You have kept the statutes of Omri,
>   and all the works of the house of Ahab;
>   and you have walked in their counsels
>
> (Micah 6.16)

Jeremiah tells of the men who rejected the laws and the appeals of God:

> They did not obey or incline their ear,
> but walked in their own counsels
>
> (Jeremiah 7.24)

To walk in the counsel of the wicked is to take the advice of the wicked in the conduct of life.

ii. The good man does not stand in the way of sinners; that is to say, he does not conform to the example of sinners. The Psalmist says of the wicked man:

> He plots mischief while on his bed;
>> he sets himself in a way that is not good;
>> he spurns not evil
>
> (Psalm 36.4)

Moses hears the word of God:

> But you, stand here by me, and I will tell you all the commandment and the statutes and the ordinances which you shall teach them
>
> (Deuteronomy 5.31)

To stand with someone is to adopt his way of life.

iii. The good man does not sit in the seat of scoffers; that is to say, he never associates with those who mock at sacred things. Weiser says that the root cause of sin is when a man begins to mock God. When he does that, he does not only separate himself from God; he puts himself above God. And Weiser goes on to say that nothing has such an unsettling effect on young people as the mocking of the very things which ought to be their mainstay. Isaiah attacks those who think that they can mock God:

> Therefore hear the word of the Lord, you scoffers, who rule this people in Jerusalem! Because you have said: 'We have made a covenant with death and with Sheol we have an agreement; when the overwhelming scourge passes through, it will not come to us; for we have made lies our refuge, and in falsehood we have taken shelter'
>
> (Isaiah 28.14, 15)

These are men who have made what they think is a deal with wickedness in order to make a mock of God. God's man will never keep the company of cynical unbelievers.

The good man avoids the company and refuses the advice of three different kinds of sinners.

He does not accept the counsel of the *wicked* (*rasha*). This is the commonest and most general word for wicked. It has been suggested that the primary idea of the word is unrest, unease, restless dispeace. Isaiah writes:

> The wicked are like the tossing sea;
>> for it cannot rest,
>> and its waters toss up mire and dirt.
> There is no peace, says my God, for the wicked
>
>> (Isaiah 57.20, 21)

If this is the basic meaning of the word, it speaks of the disharmony which sin causes, disharmony with God, disharmony with our fellow men and disharmony in our own heart and mind.

The good man does not stand in the way of *sinners* (*chatta*). This word denotes a missing of the mark, a mistaking of the way. The sinner is the man who misses the target he might have reached and could have reached. It may be that we should go a little further than this. It is no discredit to a man to take to himself a high aim, the highest of aims, and not quite to achieve it. It is better to fail in a great attempt than never to make the attempt; and maybe the sin is not so much to fail to reach the target as to be unaware that there is a target to reach. It is better to reach for the stars and not quite get there than to be unaware that there are stars to reach for.

The good man does not keep company with the *scoffers* (*letz*). This word denotes arrogant and cynical contempt. The Book of Proverbs has a great deal to say about the scoffer, the scorner. Scoffer is the name of the proud, haughty man, who acts with arrogant pride (Proverbs 21.24). He is the man who has no use for knowledge. 'How long will scoffers delight in their scoffing, and fools hate knowledge' (Proverbs 1.22). He is quite unteachable because he knows it all already; he is beyond the reach of discipline and reproof.

> He who corrects a scoffer gets himself abuse,
>   and he who reproves a wicked man incurs injury.
> Do not reprove a scoffer, or he will hate you;
>   reprove a wise man and he will love you
>
> (Proverbs 9.7, 8)

A scoffer does not listen to rebuke (Proverbs 13.1). He is unable to learn; he seeks wisdom in vain (Proverbs 14.6). He hates to be reproved and he will not go to the wise for advice (Proverbs 15.12). He is to be banished from society, for he is a trouble-maker. Eject him and quarrelling and abuse will go with him (Proverbs 22.10). The scoffer is the arrogant, cynical, unteachable trouble-maker who resents and refuses all discipline.

Verse 2   WHAT THE GOOD MAN LOVES

but his delight is in the law of the Lord,
and on his law he meditates day and night.

The delight of the good man is in the law of God. The word for law is *torah*, and it is difficult to translate. It means far more than mere legislation. Its basic meaning is teaching, instruction. It goes on to mean a precept or a law in which teaching is embodied. It means a body of such principles and, in particular, the Ten Commandments. But above all to the Jew the law was the Pentateuch, the first five books of the Bible. These books were the law *par excellence*: they were the very center of Scripture, so much so that the rest of the Old Testament was regarded as commentary upon them. The first five books of the Old Testament contain far more than law in the narrow legalistic sense of the term. They contain legend, story, history, poetry, prayer. The law is equated with nothing less than the word of God. Isaiah writes:

> Hear the word of the Lord,
>   you rulers of Sodom!
> Give ear to the teaching (*torah*) of our God,
>   You people of Gomorrah!

(Isaiah 1.10)

> Out of Zion shall go forth the law (*torah*),
>   and the word of the Lord from Jerusalem

(Isaiah 2.3)

The law has been defined as 'all divine revelation as the guide of life'. The law, says Weiser, is 'the intelligible expression of the divine will'; it is 'the unerring compass' by which a man is able 'to regulate his conduct'. It was the one task in life of the Scribes and Rabbis to expand and define this law, and from it to produce rules for every man in every situation of life.

The good man finds his delight in the law. As J. H. Eaton says: 'He does not accept the law with a pinched and grudging piety.' Such is his love of God, and such his trust in God, that love sweetens all obedience, and makes of the law not a burden but a delight. 'The purpose of the law,' it has been said, 'was to make men happy.' 'Happy are you, O Israel!' says Moses in Deuteronomy in his closing blessing (Deuteronomy 33.29). This note of sheer joy in the law is typical of Jewish religion at its highest. The Psalmist writes of the ordinances of the law:

> More to be desired are they than gold,
>   even much fine gold;
> sweeter also than honey
>   and drippings of the honeycomb
>
> (Psalm 19.10)

Another Psalmist speaks of the law like a lover of his loved one:

> If thy law had not been my delight,
>   I should have perished in my affliction.
> I will never forget thy precepts,
>   for by them thou hast given me life.
>
> Oh, how I love thy law!
>   It is my mediation all the day
>
> (Psalm 119.92, 93, 97)

In the thirteen basic articles of Jewish religion as formulated by Maimonides, the eighth principle is belief in the divine origin of the law, belief that both its precepts and its historical accounts were communicated by God to Moses, and the eleventh principle lays down the conviction that 'God rewards those who perform the commandments of his law, and punishes those who transgress them'. To put it vividly and pictorially, we could say that the nation of Israel had a love affair with the law. Collie Knox told how when he was young and intense, a much admired teacher said to him: 'Young Knox, don't make an agony of your religion.' Robert Burns said that he was haunted rather than helped by his religion. For the devout Jew religion was all joy.

The good man meditates on God's law day and night. In doing this, he is doing what Scripture tells him to do. 'This book of the law shall not depart out of your mouth, but you shall meditate on it day and night' (Joshua 1.8).

> When I think of thee upon my bed,
>> and meditate on thee in the watches of the night
>>> (Psalm 63.6)

> I remember the days of old,
>> I meditate on all that thou hast done;
>> I muse on what thy hands have wrought
>>> (Psalm 143.5)

The word *meditate* is interesting. It does not mean to sit silently and think about God and his law. For the Jew to meditate on the law was to read it in a low, murmuring tone. The Jew was right in this, for thus to read aloud was a great help to concentration, and also to memorization. The idea, as Weiser says, was for a man to so soak himself in the law that it pervaded his whole being, until in the end it became a second nature. The constant meditation was intended to remind a man that the will of God 'is not manifested in one commandment which could be done and finished'; God lays claim not simply to one decision but to the 'whole man' and his 'total conduct'. This is of the very essence of Jewish religion. In the Dead Sea Scrolls it is laid down:

> There is not to be absent from them (the community) one who can interpret the law to them at any time of day or night, for the harmonious adjustment of their human relationships. The general members of the community are to keep awake for a third of all the nights of the year, reading books, studying the law, and worshipping together.

The Jew was certain that, unless a man lived with the *torah*, neither his relationship with God nor with his fellow men could be right.

Verse 3   A MAN LIKE A TREE

He is like a tree
   planted by streams of water,
that yields its fruit in its season,
   and its leaf does not wither.
In all that he does, he prospers.

The good man is like a tree planted near streams of water. More correctly, the good man is like a tree transplanted into a well-watered garden. Jeremiah used exactly the same picture:

'Blessed is the man who trusts in the Lord,
   whose trust is the Lord.
He is like a tree planted by water,
   that sends out its roots by the stream,
and does not fear when heat comes,
   for its leaves remain green,
and is not anxious in the year of drought,
   for it does not cease to bear fruit'

(Jeremiah 17.7, 8)

The rivers of water were ever much to be desired compared with the aridity of the desert. In Balaam's oracle the tents and encampments of Israel are likened to gardens beside a river (Numbers 24.6). When the preacher tells of the houses he built and the gardens he made, he says: 'I made myself pools from which to water the forest of growing trees' (Ecclesiastes 2.5, 6). The picture is of a young shoot transplanted into a well-watered, rich-soiled garden in which it can grow uninterruptedly. The tree in question is the palm tree. 'The righteous flourish like the palm tree, and grow like a cedar in Lebanon' (Psalm 92.12).

Thomson in *The Land and the Book* writes eloquently of the palm tree:

The Palm grows slowly but steadily, from century to century, uninfluenced by the alterations in the seasons which affect other trees. It does not rejoice overmuch in winter's copious rains, nor does it droop under the drought and the burning sun of summer; neither heavy weights which men place upon its head, nor the importunate urgency of the wind can sway it aside from perfect uprightness . . . There it stands, looking solemnly down on the world below, and patiently yielding its large clusters of fruit from generation to generation. They bring forth fruit in old age.

Thomson reminds us of the many uses of the palm's branches. It could be carried as a sign of triumph – 'the victory palm branch'. Its branches could be woven into an arch to be placed over the coffin of the dead as it was carried to burial. So then we may use the characteristics of the palm tree to build up the picture of the good man.

i. There is in his life the stability of a tree. And that stability has a certain independence of circumstances. Let the winds blow, let the rains come, the drought burn, the palm tree stands. The good man stands erect, immovable, foursquare against all circumstances.

ii. With its stability the palm tree has gracefulness and beauty. A beautiful woman can be compared to a palm tree:

> How fair and pleasant you are,
>> O loved one, delectable maiden!
> You are stately as a palm tree,
>> and your breasts are like its clusters

> (Song of Solomon 7.6, 7)

The good man combines strength with beauty. There is a so-called goodness which is hard and unattractive; but the goodness of God's man is a lovely thing.

iii. There is growth in the tree; it is not static. The good man grows in knowledge and in grace. Life for him is never at a standstill; it is always for him onward and upward.

iv. There is fruit from the tree. Barnes in his commentary singles out as the essential of the tree and of the good man the two qualities of permanence and productiveness. The good man is useful to his fellow men and useful to God. This usefulness is not a thing of physical strength or even of physical well-being. A person might be confined to a chair or to a bed and still have the gift of effective prayer, of creative listening, of thinking and discovering and talking.

v. The tree has its source of nourishment and so has the good man. The tree draws its strength from the streams of water. Eaton speaks of the good man 'drawing up the grace of God through the roots of his being in his meditation'. He is good and useful because he has a strength which is not his own, because to his own human effort he has added divine guidance and divine grace.

vi. The good man is a man for all seasons. The branch of the palm may be used to wave in victory or to make a shade for grief. The good man will weep with those that weep and rejoice with those who rejoice; he will be able to share both in laughter and in tears.

vii. The palm tree goes on bearing fruit in its old age. For the good man the best is always yet to be. Age will have its opportunities no less than youth. So long as he lives, life in the real sense of the term will never be at an end.

Verses 4, 5 THE FATE OF THE WICKED

> [4] *The wicked are not so,*
>   *but are like chaff which the wind drives away.*
> [5] *Therefore the wicked will not stand in the judgment,*
>   *nor sinners in the congregation of the righteous;*

The wicked will end like the chaff which the wind carries away. The chaff is a frequent Old Testament picture of the fate of the wicked. Hosea has a wonderful series of pictures about those who worship idols:

> Therefore they shall be like the morning mist
>   or like the dew that goes early away,
> like the chaff which swirls from the threshing floor
>   or like smoke from a window

(Hosea 13.3)

Zephaniah appeals to the shameless nation to mend its ways,

> before you are driven away
>   like the drifting chaff

(Zephaniah 2.2)

Israel's foes, the multitude of the ruthless, will be like passing chaff (Isaiah 29.5). It is the vivid prayer of the Psalmist for his enemies:

> Let them be like chaff before the wind,
>   with the angel of the Lord driving them on!

(Psalm 35.5)

The wicked are

> like straw before the wind,
>   and like chaff that the storm carries away

(Job 21.18)

The threshing floor was usually on a low hill outside the village in an exposed place to catch the wind. Threshing and winnowing were usually done in the late afternoon, when the sea breeze from the west was sufficiently strong to disperse the chaff but not to damage the grain. The sheaves were laid on the ground. The great wooden sled was drawn over them. This crushed the stalks and broke open the ears of grain. The crushed stalks and ears were then tossed up with the winnowing shovel. The crushed straw and the empty husks, that is, the chaff, were blown away; the heavier grain fell to the ground and was collected. The chaff was literally scattered to the four winds of heaven and vanished from sight. Just as the tree gave us the picture of the good man, so the chaff gives us the picture of the character and destiny of the evil man.

i. The chaff is empty and worthless, good for nothing. The wicked man has nothing to offer but his wickedness. He has no fruit; he is of no use in the world, useless to society and to his fellow men.

ii. The chaff is impermanent and unstable. The wind cannot harm the tree but it destroys the chaff. Wickedness may seem to flourish for the moment but it has no future.

iii. The chaff is doomed to separation. The time will come when the wicked will be weeded out by the judgment and the action of God.

iv. The wicked like the chaff are doomed to destruction. The end of the chaff is the fire or the wind. At the end of the day the wicked will be totally eliminated. It may well be that the Psalmist sees for them not punishment but obliteration, which to the ancient mind was worse.

The wicked will not *stand* in the judgment. To stand in the judgment means to survive the judgment, to be found not guilty, to have a verdict given in one's favor. 'The boastful,' says the

Psalmist to God, 'may not stand before thy eyes' (Psalm 5.5).

> If thou, O Lord, shouldst mark iniquities,
> Lord, who could stand?

(Psalm 130.3)

If God chose mercilessly to carry out judgment, none could be found not guilty. Nahum asks in regard to God:

> Who can stand before his indignation?
> Who can endure the heat of his anger?

(Nahum 1.6)

Malachi demands:

> Who can endure the day of his coming,
> and who can stand when he appears?

(Malachi 3.2)

The judgment is not necessarily the last judgment. There is a sense in which every day is a day of judgment and the Old Testament is full of stories about how God's hand smote the guilty, as, for instance, when the earth swallowed up Korah, Dathan and Abiram for their irreverence (Numbers 16). When God chooses to execute judgment, the wicked cannot survive it. Nor have the wicked any place in the assembly of the righteous, that which the Psalmist elsewhere calls 'the company of the upright' (111.1). When God assembles and collects his own people, the wicked will not be there.

Verse 6   THE TWO WAYS

for the Lord knows the way of the righteous,
but the way of the wicked will perish.

God knows the way of the righteous but the way of the wicked leads to destruction. When God is said to *know* something, it means more than that he is merely aware of it. The divine knowledge has in it either approval and care and guidance, or rejection and abandonment and judgment. The prophet Nahum writes:

> The Lord is good,
>> a stronghold in the day of trouble;
>> he knows those who take refuge in him
>
> (Nahum 1.7)

The Pastoral Epistles have it: 'The Lord knows those who are his' (II Timothy 2.19). God knows, protects and guides the way of the righteous; but the way of the wicked leads only to disaster.

It is significant that the Bible thinks regularly of religion as a way. Religion for the biblical writers is not a creed, not a theology, not a system; it is a way of life. As the Bible sees it, a man must be on his way to somewhere. So there is the way of the wicked and the wicked way (Proverbs 4.29; Psalm 138.24). There is the false way, the way of lying and falsehood and deception and delusion (Psalm 119.29, 104). There is the way which, however superficially attractive it may appear to be, is the way to death (Proverbs 14.12). There is the way of the precepts, the statutes, the commandments of God (Psalm 119.27, 32, 33). There is the way which leads to peace (Isaiah 59.8). There is the eternal way, the way which is everlasting, or perhaps, as the NEB has it, the ancient way (Psalm 139.24). There is the way of life, the way which comes from obedience and which is ever ready to pay heed to the warnings and the reproofs of God (Proverbs 6.23; 12.28; Psalm 16.11). And it is to be noted that the first name the Christian religion ever had was The Way (Acts 9.9; 19.9, 23). From the beginning to the end religion is regarded as a matter of the will as well as of the heart, as a matter of action as well as of thought, as a matter of conduct as well as of belief. A man is walking either the way to life or the way to death; either walking towards God or away from him.

This Psalm raises questions, but the questions once raised lead to their own answers.

i. It has nothing about prayer, nothing about the sacraments, nothing about sacrifice. The one thing that it does stress as the way to salvation is the study of the law. This seems on the face of it a grave deficiency; but there are two things we do well to remember. First, no one can live the Christian life without knowing what the Christian life is, no one can obey the commandments of God without knowing what they are; and, when we are faced with the height of this life and the greatness of these commandments, we must at once be driven to find the strength which is not in ourselves. Even if it does not take us to the end of the way, this Psalm certainly takes us to its beginning.

ii. As we saw at the beginning of our study, this Psalm sees things in terms of black and white. The one way is utterly right and the other utterly wrong; the one man is completely good and the other completely bad. We are apt to see things much more in terms of compromise. We are apt to say that, as the old saying has it, 'there is so much bad in the best of us and so much good in the worst of us, that it ill becomes any of us to find fault with the rest of us'. G. K. Chesterton once said that one of the main characteristics of this age is that it no longer sees things in terms of black and white; it tends to see them in terms of an indeterminate gray. It is significant that the semitic languages have no word for compromise; and that to the semitic mind gray is not a color. It would be well if we returned to a situation – or came to it for the first time – in which we realized that right is right and wrong is wrong.

iii. The Psalm thinks in terms of rewards and punishment, and the rewards are for the most part material rewards which are to come in this life. There are certain things to be said.

It is true that the Old Testament thinks very often in terms of material reward. It has been said that prosperity is the blessing of the Old Testament and adversity is the blessing of the New Testament. The Psalmist writes:

> I have been young, and now am old;
>> yet I have not seen the righteous forsaken
>> or his children begging bread
>
> (Psalm 37.25)

Proverbs is full of the idea of material reward.

> My son, do not forget my teaching,
>> but let your heart keep my commandments;
> for the length of days and years of life
>> and abundant welfare will they give you.
>
> ...
>
> Honor the Lord with your substance
>> and with the first fruits of all your produce;
> then your barns will be filled with plenty,
>> and your vats will be bursting with wine.
>
> ...
>
> Long life is in her right hand;
>> in her left hand are riches and honor
>
>> (Proverbs 3.1-2, 9, 10, 16)

> Riches and honor are with me,
>> enduring wealth and prosperity.
>
> ...
>
> I walk in the ways of righteousness,
>> in the paths of justice,

> endowing with wealth those who love me,
>> and filling their treasuries

> (Proverbs 8.18, 20, 21)

The rewards are promised as if they automatically followed goodness; but there are at least four things to be said.

First, the men who wrote the Psalms were well aware that things were by no means as simple as that. The Bible has many examples of the man who was conscious of his own goodness and utterly bewildered by what had befallen him:

> I was envious of the arrogant,
>> when I saw the prosperity of the wicked.
> For they have no pangs;
>> their bodies are sound and sleek.
> They are not in trouble as other men are;
>> they are not stricken like other men.
> Therefore pride is their necklace;
>> violence covers them as a garment.
> All in vain I have kept my heart clean
>> and washed my hands in innocence.
> For all day long I have been stricken,
>> and chastened every morning

> (Psalm 73.3-6, 13-14)

Malachi hears the charge of God against the people who have lost their confidence and lost their loyalty:

> You have said, It is vain to serve God. What is the good of our keeping his charge or of walking as in mourning before the Lord of Hosts? Henceforth we deem the arrogant blessed; evildoers not only prosper, but, when they put God to the test, they escape

> (Malachi 3.14-15)

It may be that the writer of the first Psalm had none of the doubts and the questionings, but the writers of the Bible were no strangers to the bitter experience of apparently unrewarded fidelity and blatantly successful sin.

Second, it is to be remembered that in the Old Testament there is only the most shadowy belief in any life beyond death. To this subject we shall return. It is sufficient to note at the moment that in Old Testament times the general belief was that all men after death went to Sheol, which was a shadowy, colorless land, where the shades lived a spectral existence, if existence it could be called, separated alike from God and men.

> Dost thou work wonders for the dead?
>   Do the shades rise up to praise thee?
> Is thy steadfast love declared in the grave,
>   or thy faithfulness in Abaddon?
> Are thy wonders known in the darkness,
>   or thy saving help in the land of forgetfulness?
>
> (Psalm 88.10-12)

> The dead do not praise the Lord,
>   nor do any that go down into silence
>
> (Psalm 115.17)

The plain fact of Jewish religion at this stage was that, if God was going to vindicate his people at all, it had to be in this world for there was no real life after death.

Third, this whole confidence in the will and power of God to reward his own is what Barnes calls 'a paean on the eternal righteousness of God'. It is the unhesitating, undoubting statement that no man can lose with God. As Weiser puts it: 'Because God is God, it is impossible that anything can fail which man does in obedient execution of the will of God . . . The true meaning and value of life is to be found not in success as such but in that joyous and unshakable trust in God which cannot be broken, and the only way that leads to that goal is precisely the obedience rendered by faith.' The certainty of the reward of the righteous and the punishment of the wicked is nothing other than a tremendous affirmation of trust in the love, the justice and the power of God.

Fourth, in two directions truly Christian doctrine develops this teaching about rewards and punishments. First, it sees that the real reward lies not in money or in any material thing. It lies in the joy which is like no other, the joy of having done the right thing. It lies in the peace which is like no other, the peace of having a conscience at rest and of being able to look God and man in the face. Second, once Christianity has assured men of a life to come, a new dimension has been added. It means that God has all eternity to work in and a new world can be called in to redress the balance of the old.

The true confidence is the confidence in the justice and love of God; the true reward is the peace and satisfaction of having done the right thing with God.

iv. One last difficulty meets us. This Psalm seems to teach an absolute separation between the good and the bad, between the man whose heart is set on God and the man who has lost his soul to the world. The principle is that you cannot touch pitch and not be defiled and that evil communications must corrupt good manners. This is the principle which made the Pharisee what his name means – The Separated One. This is what made him twitch his robe aside lest it should touch an ordinary man, made him refuse to be a guest at the house of an ordinary person or have him as a guest in his house, made him refuse even to journey with an ordinary person, made him thank God that he was not as other men are (Luke 18.9-14). It is the very opposite of the principle that made Jesus the friend of the outcasts, with whom the respectable would have nothing to do (Matthew 9.9-13; Luke 15.1, 2). Just two things have to be said. First, everything depends on why we company with the man who will have nothing to do with God. Is it because we wish to be like him or because we want to change him? Is it because we have a half-hidden desire to share his life or because we want him to share the secret which is ours? Second, everything depends on how strong we are. Have we the strength of will to resist the temptations involved? Have we the moral courage and power to walk with the world and yet keep our garments unspotted from it? The Christian cannot isolate himself from the world; but before he plunges into it, he must be sure that he wants to change it, not conform to it, and he must be equally sure that he so loves his fellow men and so loves purity that he will change them and not they him.

Weiser sums up the aim of this Psalm as being three-fold; it endeavours to guide, to educate and to press for a decision. It appeals for the knowledge and the trust which will stake everything on God.

Psalm 2

GOD IS THE LORD

Why do the nations conspire,
   and the peoples plot in vain?
2 The kings of the earth set themselves,
   and the rulers take counsel together,
   against the LORD and his anointed, saying,
3 'Let us burst their bonds asunder,
   and cast their cords from us.'

4 He who sits in the heavens laughs;
   the LORD has them in derision.
5 Then he will speak to them in his wrath,
   and terrify them in his fury, saying,
6 'I have set my king
   on Zion, my holy hill.'

7 I will tell of the decree of the LORD:
   He said to me, 'You are my son,
      today I have begotten you.

8 Ask of me, and I will make the nations your heritage,
   and the ends of the earth your possession.
9 You shall break them with a rod of iron,
   and dash them in pieces like a potter's vessel.'

10 Now therefore, O kings, be wise;
   be warned, O rulers of the earth.
11 Serve the LORD with fear,
   with trembling[12] kiss his feet,*a*

lest he be angry, and you perish in the way;
for his wrath is quickly kindled.

Blessed are all who take refuge in him.

THE KING'S CORONATION

This Psalm has three possible backgrounds. It could come from
any one of them and it could come from all three.

i. This could be a Psalm, as Mahood says, composed for
some particular coronation. It begins with the picture of the
nations in a turmoil of plotting and threatened rebellion. Such
a situation regularly arose when a new king came to the throne.
At such a time the subject nations regularly tried to seize their
freedom before the new king was firmly established.

If the Psalm comes from some such time in Hebrew history,
it could only be before the exile, for once the exile had come
there was no Hebrew Empire in which subject nations could
rebel; and if the Psalm is to be attached to the actual coronation
of a king, that king could only be Solomon. There is no record
of any such rebellion, but in Hadad's request to Pharaoh to be
allowed to return home we may well see an intended attempt to
seize freedom, and we do know that Hadad did Solomon
'mischief' (I Kings 11.21-25). Even then, if taken literally, the
Psalm would be a vast exaggeration, for Israel never was
anywhere near to holding a world empire.

It is known that such songs were sung at the coronation of
Assyrian and Babylonian kings; and it has been suggested that
the court poet who wrote the Psalm was writing in terms of the
great world empires, although his own land was small.

ii. Many modern scholars have found reason to believe that

at the time of their New Year, the Jews had a series of great interconnected festivals. One was the festival of the Covenant, at which they remembered the covenant God had made with their nation, reenacted it, and rededicated themselves to it. At the same time they held the festival of the Enthronement of Jahweh; and it may well be that the many Psalms which speak of Jahweh being king and Jahweh reigning were connected with that festival. 'Jahweh reigns; let the people tremble.' 'Jahweh is a great God, and a great King above all gods.' 'Thou art my King and my God.' 'God is the king of all the earth' (99.11; 97.1; 96.10; 95.3; 44.4; 47.7; 68.24; 74.12; 98.6). At the same time as Jahweh was enthroned as King of the world, the coronation ceremony of the reigning king was repeated, and he was confirmed in his royal power. This enthroning ceremony was carried out in Egypt and Babylon, but in these lands the earthly king was regarded as physically the son of God. Ezekiel condemned the prince of Tyre, because he said; 'I am a god. I sit in the seat of the gods' (Ezekiel 28.2).

It could then be that this Psalm was one of those which were sung every year at the re-enthronement of the king; not attached to any one coronation but symbolic of all kingship and used regularly at the annual commemoration of the king's accession.

iii. The third possibility is that the Psalm is Messianic. It is true that Cyrus speaks of himself as 'the king of the world'; but, wide as his empire was, not even he could seriously claim that title. At no time in history could the Jews have thought in political terms of having the nations for their inheritance.

God's promise had been made to Israel and to her king. No king had ever entered into the promise or ever fulfilled the hopes. But the promise was God's and it stood. What could not happen by human means must happen by divine, and so it may be that the king of which this Psalm is thinking is the Messiah and the empire the Messiah's universal kingdom.

Certainly the New Testament did not hesitate to apply it to Jesus 'Thou art my Son, today I have begotten thee', is applied to Jesus in connection with his resurrection in Paul's speech at Antioch (Acts 13.33); also by the writer of the Letter to the Hebrews to distinguish him from the Angels (Hebrews 1.5). The picture of the raging Gentiles and the embattled kings and rulers is applied to the crucifying of Jesus (Acts 4.25-28). The picture of ruling with the rod of iron is applied to Jesus in Revelation 12.5 and 19.5. What was true of no earthly king would be true of the Messiah.

So the Psalm can come from the background of a king's coronation, or from the background of the annual festival at which the king's enthronement was commemorated, or it can be looking beyond history to the time and triumph of the Messiah. The Psalm falls into four equal stanzas.

In the first stanza, verses 1-3, the Psalmist sees with astonishment the nations seizing the occasion of the coronation of the new king as an opportunity to revolt.

In the second stanza, verses 4-6, the scene shifts to heaven, where God is amused at the antics of little men, and prepares to blast them with his word.

In the third stanza, verses 7-9, the king cites his credentials. When he became king he became the adopted son of God. What greater status could he have? He has the promises of God. What further resources does he need?

In the fourth stanza, verses 10 and 11, the Psalmist appeals to the rebellious ones to drop their folly before they are irreparably ruined.

Finally, in a line which is a kind of epilogue the Psalmist lays it down that the only true refuge is God.

Verses 1-3 THE FOLLY OF THE NATIONS

Why do the nations conspire,
  and the peoples plot in vain?
The kings of the earth set themselves,
  and the rulers take counsel together,
  against the Lord and his anointed, saying,
'Let us burst their bonds asunder,
  and cast their cords from us.'

The nations are the *goyim*, and the *goyim* are in contrast with Israel; and, since such nations are frequently hostile to Israel and opposed to Jahweh, the word can often mean something like 'heathen' in distinction to Israel with its true religion and its pure worship.

We have already seen the background of the Psalm. A new king has come to the throne and, as regularly happened in any empire, the subject nations are trying to use the period of transition to break away and seize their freedom. The immortal music of Handel's *Messiah* has stamped the words of the AV on the memory:

Why do the nations rage, and the people imagine a vain thing?

There is a turmoil of conspiracy and plots. The word which is used in verse 1 for to *imagine* or as the RSV has it better, to *plot*, is the same word as is used for to *meditate* in Psalm 1.2. A man may use his mind to think the thoughts of God or to plan rebellion against God. The very language used tells us two things about these plans for rebellion. *Why* do the nations conspire? It is *causeless*. And what they plot is *in vain*; it is what the NEB calls *futile plots*; it is hopeless. Rebellion against God is causeless and hopeless.

'The kings of the earth' is a phrase which the writer of the Revelation used more than once to describe earthly potentates

in contradistinction to God, the King of kings. The kings of the
earth will seek to hide themselves in the day of the wrath of God
(Revelation 6.15). The kings of the earth are under the
domination of the great harlot and have committed fornication
with her (Revelation 17.2, 18; 18.3, 9). The kings of the earth
are against God in the final battle (Revelation 19.19); but in the
end they will bring their glory to the Holy City and to the Lamb
(Revelation 21.24).

The kings of the earth are in contradistinction to the king
whom in verse 6 God calls *his king*. They *set themselves* against
the Lord and his anointed. They stand ready (NEB); they rise in
revolt (Jer. B); they take their stand at the head of their forces
and prepare for the pitched battle. The kings of the earth stand
for all the earthly forces which despise and defy God.

It is against Jahweh that the kings and the rulers plot. This
would be taken quite literally, for a nation's god was completely
involved in the nation's struggles, and victory and defeat
applied to him as much as to the nation. In the old days, in the
time of Jephthah, when Israel had defeated the Amorites and
occupied their territory, Israel said to her defeated foes: 'Will
you not possess what Chemosh your God gives you to possess?
And all that Jahweh our God has dispossessed before us, we will
possess?' (Judges 11.24). In the time of Hezekiah, when the
Assyrians were threatening Jerusalem, the message of the
Assyrians was: 'Do not listen to Hezekiah when he misleads you
by saying, Jahweh will deliver us. Has any of the gods of the
nations ever delivered his land out of the hand of the king of
Assyria? Where are the gods of Hamath and Arpad? Where are
the gods of Sepharvaim, Hena and Ivvah? Have they delivered
Samaria out of my hand? Who among all the gods of the
countries have delivered their countries out of my hand, that
Jahweh should deliver Jerusalem out of my hand?' (II Kings
18.31-35). To rebel against a king was literally to rebel against

the god of that king, and to rebel against Jahweh's anointed was to rebel against Jahweh.

The threatened rebellion is against Jahweh and his anointed. Jahweh's anointed was God's consecrated representative, that is, the king. Anointing was consecration to God of things or of people by pouring sacred oil upon them. So the altar could be anointed (Exodus 29.36); the tent of meeting (the tabernacle) and the ark of the testimony were both anointed (Exodus 30.26). Three kinds of people in particular were anointed. Kings were anointed, as Samuel anointed Saul, and later David (I Samuel 10.1; 16.3). Solomon was anointed by Zadok (I Kings 1.39), as was Jehu by one of the sons of the prophets (II Kings 9.6). Priests were anointed; they were to be anointed and ordained and consecrated that they might serve God (Exodus 28.41). Prophets were anointed. Elijah was to anoint Elisha as his successor (I Kings 19.16). The anointed ones were not to be touched and the prophets were not to be harmed (I Chronicles 16.22; Psalm 105.15).

The aim of the rebellious is to burst the bonds and throw away the cords. The bonds were the fastenings by which the yoke was attached to the neck of the ox, and the cords were the reins by which the ox was guided. Hosea hears God say:

> I led them with cords of compassion,
>   with the bands of love

(Hosea 11.4)

The idea is that of guidance and direction rather than that of restraint and subjugation.

Verses 4 6   GOD'S IN HIS HEAVEN

He who sits in the heavens laughs;
  the Lord has them in derision.

> *Then he will speak to them in his wrath,*
>   *and terrify them in his fury, saying,*
> *'I have set my king on Zion, my holy hill.'*

The scene now switches from earth to heaven. In heaven God sees the antics of men on earth and prepares to deal with them. The God of high heaven is also the God whose eye sees all that goes on on earth.

> The Lord's throne is in heaven;
>   his eyes behold, his eyelids test,
>   the children of men

> > > > (Psalm 11.4)

Sometimes the two things are marvellously put together:

> The Lord is high above all nations,
>   and his glory above the heavens!
> Who is like the Lord our God,
>   who is seated on high,
> who looks far down
>   upon the heavens and the earth?
> He raises the poor from the dust,
>   and lifts the needy from the ash heap,
> to make them sit with princes,
>   with the princes of his people.
> He gives the barren woman a home,
>   making her the joyous mother of children

> > > > (Psalm 113.4-9)

The God of high heaven is the God who cares for the poor and is kind to the childless woman.

Then comes a terrifying scene – the picture of the laughter of God. God looks down on the antics of these little men and laughs. To recognize the true importance of things and people we must see them in the sight of God; and then we will see that the things which seem important to us and the people who seem so important to themselves are nothing more than a bad joke in the sight of God.

The Old Testament writers were never afraid of anthropomorphism, that is, of attributing human thoughts and feelings to God. God, as they put it, can regret his own actions and be sorry that he ever created man (Genesis 6.6). God can love and hate: 'I have loved Jacob but I have hated Esau' (Malachi 1.2, 3). God can forget: 'Since you have forgotten the law of your God, I also will forget your children' (Hosea 4.6). The Old Testament writers tell their story with a vivid childlike simplicity of which modern man is afraid.

Then God, as it were, calls a halt. He will speak to them in his wrath – and the words of God are more than sounds in the air. They are mightily effective. It was by his word that God created the world and all that is in it (Genesis 1.3, 6, 9, 14, 20, 24, 26). 'Is not my word like fire, says the Lord, and like a hammer which breaks the rock in pieces?' (Jeremiah 23.29). 'He shall smite the earth with the rod of his mouth, and with the breath of his lips he shall slay the wicked' (Isaiah 11.4). God's word does what he sends it to do (Isaiah 55.11); it is not a mere protest. So God speaks in his wrath. The word used for wrath is hardly ever used of anyone else but God; it really means *fiery wrath*:

> In the greatness of thy majesty
> thou overthrowest thy adversaries;
> thou sendest forth thy fury,
> it consumes them like stubble

(Exodus 15.7)

God terrifies them with his fury. Here, says Weiser, we hear the far-off rumblings of the thunder of judgment.

Verse 6 is more emphatic in the Hebrew than in the English – 'It is *I* who have set my king on Zion, my holy hill.' Zion was the name of the ancient stronghold which was to become Jerusalem the Holy City. It was not in Jerusalem, it was in Hebron, that David was installed as king (II Samuel 2.1-4). Seven years later David captured Zion and transferred his capital to it (II Samuel 5.1-9). It was not until the time of Solomon that the temple was built but by bringing the ark to Zion David made it the sacred city (II Samuel 6). So then, whatever the antics of men, God is in his heaven and is in control.

Verses 7-9   KING BY GOD'S DECREE

I will tell of the decree of the Lord;
    He said to me, 'You are my son,
    today I have begotten you.

Ask of me, and I will make the nations
        your heritage,
    and the ends of the earth your possession.
You shall break them with a rod of iron,
    and dash them in pieces like a potter's vessel.'

In the first stanza of the Psalm the scene was set; in the second stanza the scene shifted to heaven and God spoke; now in the third stanza the scene returns to earth and the speaker is the king.

The king, as it were, gives his credentials; it is by nothing less than the decree of God that he is king. That decree is expressed in the words with which the prophet Nathan conveyed to David the promise of God:

'I will give you rest from all your enemies. Moreover the Lord declares to you that the Lord will make you a house. When your days are fulfilled and you lie down with your fathers, I will raise up your offspring after you, who shall come forth from your body, and I will establish his kingdom. He shall build a house for my name, and I will establish the throne of his kingdom for ever. I will be his father and he shall be my son. When he commits iniquity, I will chasten him with the rod of men, with the stripes of the sons of men; but I will not take my steadfast love from him, as I took it from Saul, whom I put away from before you. And your house and your kingdom shall be made sure for ever before me; your throne shall be established for ever'

(II Samuel 7.11-16)

As another Psalmist has it:

He shall cry to me, Thou art my Father,
   my God, and the Rock of my salvation.
And I will make him the firstborn,
   the highest of the kings of the earth.
My steadfast love I will keep for him for ever,
   and my covenant will stand firm for him.
I will establish his line for ever
   and his throne as the days of the heavens.
Once for all I have sworn by my holiness;
   I will not lie to David.
His line shall endure for ever,
   his throne as long as the sun before me.
Like the moon it shall be established for ever;
   it shall stand firm while the skies endure

(Psalm 89.26-29, 35-37)

The promise was that the throne of David was to be as sure as the constitution of the universe.

For that reason on the day that the king came to the throne he became in a very special sense the son of God. On the coronation day God said: 'You are my son.' These words were the official adoption formula, the words a man spoke when he adopted a son. It has been pointed out that when the king became by adoption the son of God that status at one and the same time laid down the *extent* and the *limits* of his power. Being his son the power of God was available for him; but, equally, being the son of God meant that his whole life must be spent in obedience to his father. In the one word *privilege* and *duty* are inextricably combined – and what was true for the king is true for all of us.

God invites the king who is his son to claim his inheritance, 'Ask of me.' At one time the inheritance of Israel was the land of Canaan. 'I will give to you . . . the land of Canaan, for possession' (Genesis 17.8). To Moses it was forbidden to enter 'the good land which the Lord your God gives you for an inheritance' (Deuteronomy 4.21). From the top of Mount Nebo Moses was to view the land into which he could never enter, 'the land of Canaan, which I give to the people of Israel for an inheritance' (Deuteronomy 32.49). But when it became known that Jahweh was not simply the God of Israel but the God of all the earth, then the inheritance became not only Canaan but 'dominion from sea to sea and from the River (the Euphrates) to the ends of the earth!' (Psalm 72.8; Zechariah 9.9, 10).

There are two possible pictures in verse 9. The second half of the verse is quite clear. The smashing of a potter's vessel was the regular picture for a destruction which was at once easy, complete and irreparable. If the rebellious ones continued to be rebellious, their confederation could be destroyed and they could never be able to put it together again. When Jeremiah was rebuking the people for their disobedience and their sin, he took a potter's earthen flask and told them that the message of God was: 'So will I break this people and this city, as one breaks a potter's vessel, so that it can never be mended' (Jeremiah

19.11). Isaiah made the same threat: continued disobedience would bring a break like the breaking of a potter's vessel, 'which is smashed so ruthlessly that among its fragments not a sherd is found with which to take fire from the hearth, or to dip up water out of the cistern' (Isaiah 30.14). The smashing of the potter's vessel contained the threat of total disaster.

In the first half of verse 9 there are two possibilities. The threat may be that of smashing the enemies with an iron sceptre, as if an iron hand was to fall on them and so bring them to utter destruction. But the rod of iron may be also the iron-tipped rod with which the shepherd defends his flock from wild beasts and marauding foes (Psalm 23.4). And by a very small change the word *break* could become *shepherd* so that the picture would be not that of destruction with an iron hand but that of protection with the shepherd's rod. The Greek version of the Old Testament takes it the second way. W. E. Barnes suggests that the two lines of verse 9 could form a contrast:

> Thou shalt be a shepherd (to those who submit) guiding
> them with the shepherd's iron rod;
> Thou shalt dash to pieces (the others, the rebellious), as
> a potter's vessel is destroyed.

On the whole it seems more likely that here there is a double threat of destruction to those who rebel; which brings us face to face with the ever-recurring declaration of the Bible that promise and threat go constantly hand in hand.

Verses 10, 11   THE FINAL APPEAL

Now therefore, O kings, be wise;
be warned, O rulers of the earth.
Serve the Lord with fear,
with trembling kiss his feet,

> lest he be angry, and you perish in the way;
>   for his wrath is quickly kindled.

> Blessed are all who take refuge in him.

In the last two verses comes the final appeal. It may be the Psalmist himself who is making it; it may be the king; and it could even be God himself. We note one point. The AV has: 'Be instructed, ye judges of the earth.' The RSV has: 'Be warned, O rulers of the earth.' 'Learn your lesson,' says the NEB, 'you rulers of the earth.' We find frequently that the newer translations use some such word as ruler or governor where the older translations speak of judges. We have only to think of the characters in the Book of Judges to see that these men did far more than administer justice. They were the rulers of the people, the commanders of the armies, the guardians of their nation's religion and worship; but because their chief task was the administration of justice, they were called judges. It does, however, give a better idea of their function to think of them as the rulers of their country.

There is clearly a great deal of uncertainty about the exact form of verse 11 (11 and 12 in the AV). The AV has:

> Serve the Lord with fear, and rejoice with trembling.
> Kiss the Son, lest he be angry, and ye perish from the way,
> when his wrath is kindled but a little.

The RSV has:

> Serve the Lord with fear,
>   with trembling kiss his feet,
> lest he be angry, and you perish in the way;
>   for his wrath is quickly kindled.

The NEB has:

> Worship the Lord with reverence;
> tremble and kiss the king
> lest the Lord be angry and you are struck down in mid course;
>> for his anger flares up in a moment.

The NEB has a note that the Hebrew is obscure, and that the literal meaning is:

> Tremble and kiss the mighty one.

Kiss the Son – with trembling kiss his feet – tremble and kiss the king – kiss the mighty one – are all perfectly intelligible expressions. They depict the actual act of submission or of respect that was made to kings and conquerors. When Samuel made Saul king, he 'took a vial of oil and poured it upon his head, and kissed him' (I Samuel 10.1). God's message to the despairing Elijah was that there were still seven thousand who had not bowed the knee to Baal and whose mouth had not kissed him (I Kings 19.18). The Psalmist's prayer for the king is that 'his foes bow down before him and his enemies lick the dust' (Psalm 72.9). The promise in Isaiah is that on the great day of triumph and restoration kings and queens with their faces to the ground will bow down before them, 'and lick the dust of your feet' (Isaiah 49.23). Hosea speaks bitterly of the men who kiss calves, the idols of Samaria (Hosea 13.2). The picture is clear and common enough. But three difficulties are raised.

First, some scholars feel that the AV's phrase, 'Rejoice with trembling', is a contradiction in terms because, they say, trembling and rejoicing cannot be united. W. E. Barnes feels the very opposite. 'Rejoice with trembling' is, he says, 'perhaps the noblest description which could be given of the attitude of the truly religious man'. Barnes is right. Surely there is a joy touched with such wonder and reverence and love that it becomes a tremulous thing.

Second, and this is a real difficulty, the word for *son* in 'Kiss the Son' is *bar*, which is a late word for *son*; the classical word for *son* is *ben*, which is actually used in verse 7. So, it is felt, this phrase cannot stand.

Third, the Greek translation of the Psalms, and the Jewish Targum, both have a quite different expression – 'Lay hold of instruction.' The word *bar* which, if taken to mean *son*, causes problems, can also mean *pure* or *chosen*. So the meaning could be, 'Worship the chosen one', 'Pay homage to the pure one'.

The difficulties are no more than incidental. The essential meaning is that those who threaten rebellion are being urged to submit in reverence and humility to him who is God's vice-regent on earth. And let them make their submission quickly or even on the road the wrath of God may catch up on them.

So the Psalm ends with peace – Blessed are all who take refuge in him – as if to invite men to the peace of God after the storms of passion and self-will. It is not surprising that this Psalm became a very special and very precious possession of the Christian Church. It is repeatedly quoted in the New Testament. The raging of the peoples and the kings is used as a forecast of the crucifixion of Jesus (Acts 4.25-27). 'You are my son' is repeatedly used of Jesus – in regard to his resurrection (Acts 13.33); as a proof that he is greater than any of the angels (Hebrews 1.5); as the proof of his qualification as the perfect high priest (Hebrews 5.5). The promise of the rule with the rod of iron is regularly used of the reign of the Messiah in the Revelation (2.26, 27; 12.5; 19.15). In the Revelation the phrase 'the kings of the earth' is repeatedly used of human as contrasted with divine power (1.5; 6.15; 16.14; 17.2; 18; 18.3; 9; 19.19; 21.24).

Weiser said that the Psalm has only one aim – 'to show that God is the Lord, and to make sure that he will be recognized as such'.

The astonishing thing about this Psalm, the thing to which the mind insists on returning, is its defiance of the facts. Israel was a tiny nation, her king a petty king, but she never doubted her ultimate destiny. The Jew was certain that it was better to be agonizingly right with God than prosperously wrong with heathen nations who neither knew nor cared for God. It is a choice that comes sometimes to every individual and nation – to take the easy immediate wrong or the costly ultimate right? James Russell Lowell's poem *The Present Crisis* is still relevant.

> So the Evil's triumph sendeth, with a terror and a chill,
> Under continent to continent, the sense of coming ill.

What then?

> Though the cause of Evil prosper, yet 'tis truth alone is strong.
> Truth for ever on the scaffold, Wrong for ever on the throne, –
> Yet that scaffold holds the future, and behind the dim unknown,
> Standeth God within the shadow keeping watch above
>   His own.

> Then to side with Truth is noble when we share her wretched
>   crust,
> Ere her cause bring fame and profit, and 'tis prosperous to be
>   just;
> Then it is the brave man chooses, while the coward stands
>   aside,
> Doubting in his abject spirit, till his Lord is crucified.

If God is God then ultimately truth must prevail. In his opera *Princess Ida* W. S. Gilbert wrote some lines which are sung by Lady Blanche. Lady Blanche's dreams and ambitions have never been fulfilled, but she is sure that they will be:

> Come, mighty Must!
> Inevitable Shall!

In thee I trust.
Time weaves my coronal!
Go, mocking Is!
Go, disappointing Was!

Away! The Mighty Must
Shall be!

Gilbert was no great poet, and he is best known as a writer of comic operas, but this time he struck a chord of eternal truth: God's mighty Must shall be! – and that is the meaning of this Psalm.

Psalm 8

GOD AND MAN

Psalm 8 is another Psalm in praise of God. Its theme is the frailty of man contrasted with the majestic glory of God, and the place which God has given to man in his creation, in spite of man's insignificance.

O LORD, our Lord,
how majestic is thy name in all the earth!

Thou whose glory above the heavens is chanted
2   by the mouth of babes and infants,
thou hast founded a bulwark because of thy foes,
to still the enemy and the avenger.

3 When I look at thy heavens, the work of thy fingers,
the moon and the stars which thou hast established;
4 what is man that thou art mindful of him,
and the son of man that thou dost care for him?

5 Yet thou hast made him little less than God,
and dost crown him with glory and honor.
6 Thou hast given him dominion over the works of thy hands;
thou hast put all things under his feet,
7 all sheep and oxen,
and also the beasts of the field,
8 the birds of the air, and the fish of the sea,
whatever passes along the paths of the sea.

9 O LORD, our Lord,
how majestic is thy name in all the earth!

Verse 1a   THE MAJESTY OF GOD

O Lord, our Lord,
  how majestic is thy name in all the earth!

The two *Lords* are different words in the Hebrew. The first is
Jahweh; the second is Adonai. So strictly the translation should
be: 'O Jahweh, our Lord.' The RSV does not mark the
difference nor does the TEV. Coverdale in the Prayer Book
Version of the Psalms did mark it by translating: 'O Lord, our
Governor', and the NEB preserves the difference by translating:
'O Lord, our sovereign.' The Psalm ends with the same two lines
as it begins with; the beginning and the end of the Psalmist's
thought is the majesty of God.

The AV has: 'How excellent is thy name in all the earth!'
Excellent is used in its literal sense – excelling all others; it
means majestic, mighty, glorious, splendid, magnificent.

The Hebrew writers used the expression *thy name* in a
special way. 'How majestic is thy name!' clearly does not mean
that there is anything very splendid about the name Jahweh.
Another Psalmist says:

> Those who know thy name put their trust in thee
>
> (Psalm 9.10)

Clearly this cannot mean that those who know that God's name
is Jahweh put their trust in him. Still another says:

> Some boast of chariots, and some of horses:
>   but we boast of the name of Jahweh our God
>
> (Psalm 20.7)

This cannot mean that they boast because their God is called
Jahweh.

In Hebrew the *name* of God is used for the character of God
as far as that character can be seen from the works of creation

and the events of history. So, if the Psalmist says, 'Those who know thy name put their trust in thee', he means that those who know what God is like have no hesitation in putting their trust in him. So what the writer of Psalm 8 is saying is: 'O Jahweh, our Lord, how glorious and majestic your whole world shows your character and nature to be.'

Verses 1b-4   THE INSIGNIFICANCE OF MAN

Thou whose glory above the heavens is chanted
  by the mouth of babes and infants,
thou hast founded a bulwark because of thy foes,
  to still the enemy and the avenger.

When I look at thy heavens, the work of thy fingers,
  the moon and the stars which thou hast established;
what is man that thou art mindful of him,
  and the son of man that thou dost care for him?

The Hebrew original of the first four lines is uncertain. There are at least four possible translations each of which has something of value to say.

i. There is the translation of the RSV and the Jerusalem Bible:

Thou whose glory above the heavens is chanted,
  by the mouths of babes and infants,
thou hast founded a bulwark because of thy foes,
  to still the enemy and the avenger.

This has two possible meanings.

(a) It can mean that the God whose glory out-stretches the heavens accepts also the praise of the little child. This is the way in which Jesus quotes it in Matthew. When the children sang their Hosannas on the day Jesus entered Jerusalem, the orthodox authorities were offended, and Jesus said: 'Yes, have you never read:

> Out of the mouths of babes and sucklings
> thou hast brought perfect praise?'
>
> (Matthew 21.16)

This is also the translation of the Septuagint, the Greek version of the Old Testament.

(b) In modern times it has been suggested that babes and infants is a traditional phrase for the heavenly beings who are children of God. So there is an Eastern writing which speaks of 'the gracious gods . . . who suck the nipples of Asherah's breasts'. In that case, the babes and infants are, so to speak, heavenly babes and infants – and it is a possible, even if unlikely, meaning.

ii. There is the translation of the NEB:

> Thy majesty is praised high as the heavens.
> Out of the mouth of babes, of infants at the breast,
>   thou hast rebuked the mighty,
>   silencing enmity and vengeance to teach thy foes a lesson.

In this translation the punctuation is different. A full stop comes at the end of the first line. The babes and infants are not connected with praise, but it is said that out of their mouth the mighty are rebuked. Here is the teaching that the little child can rebuke and even overcome the mighty. Weiser writes of the effect of a little child: 'Even the adversaries (sceptics and atheists) cannot disregard the fact that the child utterly and completely surrenders to the impression produced by things which are great and glorious, and does so in an unaffected and direct manner, albeit he expresses his wonder in a childlike and halting fashion, and gives expression to his childlike joy in the works of God's creation by his games and songs . . . They cannot disregard those first stirrings of a naïve and unreflecting piety which are after all a fact.' 'How often,' he says, 'are the trains of thought of adults put to shame by the unfeigned purity of the feelings expressed in the words of a little child?' 'A little child shall lead them,' says Isaiah, speaking even of the untamable beasts (Isaiah 11.6). And Jesus himself said that unless a man became as a little child he could not enter the kingdom of heaven (Matthew 18.1-4). A famous author spoke of seeing his little son lying in bed on a morning 'worshipping the sunbeam on the bed-post'. The faith of a child, the trust of a child, the simplicity of a child, the love of a child, the joy of a child, a child's wonder at nature and its loveliness – these are arguments which can on occasion break down the hostility of one who himself has no belief.

iii. *Today's English Version* of the Psalms takes all the connections away:

> Your praise reaches up to the heavens;
>> it is sung by children and babies.
> You have built a fortress against your foes,
>> to stop your enemies and adversaries.

Here three simple things are said about God. First, his praise is sung in the heights of heaven. Second, his praise is sung by the little child. Third, if God has those who attack, he also has his defenses and cannot be overcome.

iv. There is the translation of Dahood in the Anchor Bible commentary on Psalms:

> I will adore your majesty above the heavens
> with the lips of striplings and sucklings.
> You built a fortress for your habitation,
>> having silenced your adversaries,
>> the foe and the avenger.

God's majesty is higher than the heavens but the Psalmist will adore it, even if his adoration has to be expressed in the lisping, stammering tongue of the stripling and the suckling. We must give what praise we can and, although it may be sadly inadequate, if it is our best, God will accept it. 'Before the majesty of God the Psalmist can but babble like an infant.'

> You built a fortress for your habitation,
>> having silenced your adversaries,
>> the foe and the avenger.

Dahood takes this to be a reference to creation. The fortress God built for himself is heaven and the adversaries are the forces of chaos which God defeated when he created the world. This then would be a reference to God's victory over chaos.

We do not need to choose between the different translations. It is not an either/or but a both/and. And here indeed is riches. God is praised by the angels and by the little child. He can break the unfaith of the mighty by the faith of a little child. He is praised in heaven and praised on earth and has his own undefeatable defence. It may be that our praise is feeble and unworthy but, such as we have, let us give. God is our Father, and a loving father never rebuffed his child's best effort.

> When I look at thy heavens, the work of thy fingers,
>> the moon and the stars which thou hast established;
> what is man that thou art mindful of him,
>> and the son of man that thou dost care for him?

In a vivid phrase the Psalmist calls the heavens the work of the fingers of God. He looks up in the Eastern night; he sees that star-scattered immensity which is the sky; and he is amazed that the God who made all that can have any thought for tiny and insignificant man. Another Psalmist says:

> The heavens are thine, the earth is also thine;
>> the world and all that is in it,
>> thou hast founded them

(Psalm 89.11)

Isaiah the prophet looks up to the heavens and sees the stars:

> Lift up your eyes on high and see: who created these?
> He who brings out their host by number,
>> calling them all by name;
> by the greatness of his might,
>> and because he is strong in power
>> not one is missing

(Isaiah 40.26)

If the Psalmist was staggered at the immensity of the heavens, how much more must we be? Distances in the universe are so great that astronomers measure them in light years. Light travels at 186,000 miles per second so that in a year it travels six million million miles. The observable universe – and how much more of it may be beyond our ken – is so vast that it would take light 30,000 million years to cross it. That is to say, the length across the observable universe is 30,000,000,000 multiplied by 6,000,000,000,000 miles. The universe is speeding through space at the rate of twelve miles per second. If we set out and traveled at twelve miles a second steadily and without stopping it would take us 60,000 years to reach the nearest star.

On a clear night with the naked eye we can see 5000 stars – that was what the Psalmist saw. With a four-inch lens telescope we could see more than 2,000,000, and with a 200-inch mirror such as there is on Mount Palomar in the United States we could see more than 1000 million.

Stars are assembled into galaxies and some of the larger galaxies are 100,000 light years in diameter. Galaxies go in pairs. The earth is in the galaxy known as the Milky Way; its pair is Andromeda, which is about 2,000,000 light years away. Galaxies are assembled into clusters and a cluster may contain 1000 galaxies, varying from 1,000,000 to 10,000,000 light years across. The clusters form groups of maybe 100 clusters spread over 100 million light years. There could be more than 100,000 million galaxies in the universe, each containing more than 100,000 million stars. Such distances are inconceivable to the ordinary mind. If the Psalmist in his day was lost in wonder at the creating power of God, how much more must we be, when we know so much more about the sky and the stars?

The Psalmist wonders how this infinite God can have any concern with puny man. The very words he uses are expressive. 'What is *man* that thou art mindful of him?' Here the word for man is *enosh*, which may mean *the weak one* and describes man in all his frailty and mortality.

> As for man (*enosh*), his days are like grass;
>> he flourishes like a flower of the field;
> for the wind passes over it, and it is gone,
>> and its place knows it no more
>
> (Psalm 103.15)

> Can mortal man (*enosh*) be righteous before God?
>
> (Job 4.17)

'And the son of man that thou dost care for him?' This use of *son of man* is quite different from Jesus' use of it. In Hebrew *son of man* means an ordinary human being, man considered as a creature of the earth, 'mere man' as TEV has it.

> God is not man that he should lie,
>> or a son of man that he should repent
>
> (Numbers 23.19)

Let thy hand be upon the man of thy right hand,
  the son of man whom thou hast made strong for thyself
                                        (Psalm 80.17)

O Lord, what is man that thou dost regard him,
  or the son of man that thou dost think of him?
                                        (Psalm 144.3)

Put not your trust in princes,
  in a son of man, in whom there is no help
                                        (Psalm 146.3)

So the Psalmist uses two phrases which contrast the frail
insignificance of man with the might, majesty and power of God.

As Weiser points out, the Psalmist is seeing man in the
perspective of God; the finite is being confronted with the
infinite, the transient with the eternal. And it is only when man
starts from his own total insignificance that he can begin to
understand the greatness of the divine miracle of the love of
God. Weiser talks of the interaction of the awe which trembles
at the thought of the majesty of the Lord of the Universe and
the joy which is filled with gratitude for the loving care of that
same God. When man sees himself in the perspective of God,
then he can and will say: 'By the grace of God I am what I am'
(1 Corinthians 15.10). Here is the combination of 'humble
reverence and joyful pride' in which alone both arrogance and
despair can be avoided.

Verses 5-9 THE PARADOX OF MAN

Yet thou hast made him little less than God,
  and dost crown him with glory and honor.
Thou hast given him dominion over the works of thy hands,
  thou hast put all things under his feet,

all sheep and oxen,
   and also the beasts of the field,
the birds of the air, and the fish of the sea,
   whatever passes along the paths of the sea.

O Lord, our Lord,
   how majestic is thy name in all the earth!

Here is the paradox of man. Frail, puny, transient, insignificant, mortal, but God has appointed him his viceroy on earth. The first half of verse 5 has been variously translated. Startlingly, the RSV has: 'Thou hast made him little less than God.' TEV says the same but in less startling form: 'You made him inferior only to yourself.' The NEB has: 'Thou hast made him little less than a god.' Dahood has something the same: 'You have made him a little less than the gods.' Eaton has: 'You have made him a little less than a celestial being'. The big difference comes in the translation of the AV, the Septuagint, the Jewish Targum, the Latin Vulgate, and the Letter to the Hebrews 2.7-9, all of which say that God has made man 'a little lower than the angels'.

The problem comes from the fact that the Hebrew word for God is *Elohim. -im* is the Hebrew *plural* ending and so, oddly enough, the word for God is plural in form. There is in the Bible an underlying line of thought which sees Jahweh as supreme among many. In the creation story it is: '*Let us* make man in *our* image, after *our* likeness' (Genesis 1.26). In the Psalms we find this thought recurring:

God has taken his place in the divine council;
   in the midst of the gods he holds judgment

(Psalm 82.1)

There is none like thee among the gods, O Jahweh

(Psalm 86.8)

> Who in the skies can be compared to Jahweh?
> Who among the heavenly beings is like Jahweh?
>
> (Psalm 89.6)

> All gods bow down before him
>
> (Psalm 97.7)

So it can be seen that there is a difficulty here. *Elohim* does mean God and therefore this can be translated: 'You have made him a little less than God.' On the other hand *Elohim* is plural, and there is an underlying thought of a kind of council of divine beings of whom God is chief, and among whom the angels are included.

> There came a day when the sons of God came to
> present themselves before Jahweh
>
> (Job 1.6)

It is possible therefore to translate this: 'You have made him a little lower than the angels; you have made him little less than a god or a celestial being.' It might well be better to translate it: 'You have made man only a little less than divine.'

However we take it, the idea is that of the creation story:

Then God said, 'Let us make man in our image, after our likeness; and let them have dominion over the fish of the sea, and over the birds of the air, and over the cattle, and over all the earth, and over every creeping thing that creeps upon the earth.' So God created man in his own image, in the image of God he created him; male and female he created them

(Genesis 1.26, 27)

Man is indeed only a little less than God, for God made him after his own likeness and in his own image; man has indeed dominion over creation, for that is why he was created. But certain things have to be noted.

i. Although the Psalm has this high view of man, it is not in praise of man but in praise of God. That indeed is the difference between Hellenistic and Hebrew thought. For the Greek, as Sophocles said (*Antigone* 332): 'Wonders are many, but none is more wonderful than man.' But for the Hebrew it is God who is the wonder. As Weiser puts it: 'In the Old Testament human dignity has no value of its own, but has value only as a gift from God.'

ii. This leads us to the second truth – man's dominion over creation is not an achievement; it is a gift. In verses 5 and 6 the subject of all the verbs is God. God made – God gave – God put all things under man's feet. All the action is God's. In Greek mythology, in at least one of its stories, man is the product of an act of rebellion. To tell the myth very summarily, Zeus in the form of a serpent seduced his own daughter Persephone and Dionysus was born for dominion over the earth. The Titans were envious and jealous; they stole the infant Dionysus, tore him limb from limb, cooked the pieces and ate them. But Athene rescued Dionysus' heart. Zeus swallowed the heart; Dionysus was reborn; the Titans were blasted by Zeus with lightning; and from their ashes arose mankind. In the Greek myth man came from rebellion against God. In the Old Testament story, man was created by God in his own likeness and received his dominion from God. Therefore man's dominion is not something to arouse pride but rather to excite gratitude.

iii. God's gift of dominion was not something into which man automatically entered; it was something for which he had to toil. God did not give man something ready made; he gave him potential. In the earliest days man's dominion was over the animals. He either destroyed them or tamed them for his service. 'Man,' said Darwin, 'even in his rudest state has become the most dominant animal that has ever appeared on this earth.'

God gave men dominion at a price. Earth bears its crops but only if the ground is tilled and the seed is sown and the crop is tended. There are metals in the ground but they must be dug for. With toil and sweat they have to be shaped and formed. Nature will reveal her secrets but only at the price of study and research and often sacrifice. God gave man dominion but it is a dominion whose potential man must make real.

iv. Further, it is a dominion which man must be wise enough to use. Man can discover and harness powers only to destroy himself. He has to learn that what God gave him he must use as God would have him use it. Man is not king; he is viceroy. Dominion and obedience must go hand in hand.

One thing remains to note about this Psalm; it has nothing to say about the Fall. It is concerned with the creation of man and not his fall, for it is telling of God's purpose for man and the destiny God gave him. That is why the Christian Church annexed this Psalm, especially the writer to the Hebrews (Hebrews 2.5-9). What man failed to do, the great Son of Man can do. In Jesus Christ man reaches his ideal and his destiny; in Jesus Christ man is what God meant him to be and therefore his is the final lordship and dominion. What man cannot do for himself Jesus Christ can do for him.

Psalm 19

GOD'S PLAN

The heavens are telling the glory of God;
    and the firmament proclaims his handiwork.
2 Day to day pours forth speech,
    and night to night declares knowledge.
3 There is no speech, nor are there words;
    their voice is not heard;
4 yet their voice goes out through all the earth,
    and their words to the end of the world.

In them he has set a tent for the sun,
5   which comes forth like a bridegroom leaving his chamber,
    and like a strong man runs its course with joy.
6 Its rising is from the end of the heavens,
    and its circuit to the end of them;
    and there is nothing hid from its heat.

7 The law of the LORD is perfect,
    reviving the soul;
the testimony of the LORD is sure,
    making wise the simple;
8 the precepts of the LORD are right,
    rejoicing the heart;
the commandment of the LORD is pure,
    enlightening the eyes;

9 the fear of the LORD is clean,
    enduring for ever;

the ordinances of the LORD are true,
    and righteous altogether.
10 More to be desired are they than gold,
    even much fine gold;
  sweeter also than honey
    and drippings of the honeycomb.

11 Moreover by them is thy servant warned;
    in keeping them there is great reward.
12 But who can discern his errors?
    Clear thou me from hidden faults.
13 Keep back thy servant also from presumptuous sins;
    let them not have dominion over me!
  Then I shall be blameless,
    and innocent of great transgression.
14 Let the words of my mouth and the meditation of my heart
  be acceptable in thy sight,
    O LORD, my rock and my redeemer.

GOD'S TWO GREAT VOLUMES

At first sight this Psalm seems to be composed of two almost completely unrelated parts. The first part, verses 1 to 6, is a magnificent poem in praise of nature. The second part, verses 7 to 11, is in praise of the law. There is a third section, verses 12 to 14, in which the Psalmist seeks the grace and help of God to keep him from inadvertent or deliberate sin. The break at the end of verse 6 seems complete. The subject changes and the meter changes. There seems to be no connection – but there is.

What the Psalmist is really talking about is the revelation of God to men. And, as Kirkpatrick says so well, God has two great volumes in which he reveals himself – Nature and Scripture. That is the connection between the two dissimilar

sections of the Psalm. The first section deals with God's
revelation of himself in nature; the second deals with his
revelation of himself in the law. As Kant said: 'The starry sky
above me and the moral law within me . . . are two things which
fill the soul with ever new and increasing admiration and
reverence.' Centuries after the Psalmist Paul was to make the
same point against those who disregarded and rebelled against
God. 'For what can be known about God is plain to them,
because God has shown it to them. Ever since the creation of
the world, his invisible nature, namely, his eternal power and
deity, has been clearly perceived in the things that have been
made. So they are without excuse' (Romans 1.19, 20). In his
world God is plain for all to see.

It was a basic belief of Israel's religion that the God who
created the world was the God who gave the law.

> For lo, he who forms the mountains, and creates the wind
>   and declares to man what is his thought;
> and makes the morning darkness,
>   and treads on the heights of the earth -
> Jahweh, the God of hosts, is his name
>
> (Amos 4.13)
>
> He who made the Pleiades and Orion,
>   and turns deep darkness into the morning,
>   and darkens the day into night,
> who calls for the waters of the sea,
>   and pours them out upon the surface of the earth,
> Jahweh is his name
>
> (Amos 5.8)

That is why the two sections of the Psalm naturally come
together – the God of creation is the God of the law. The Bible
and the world are each his self-revelation.

Verses 1, 2 NATURE'S CEASELESS HYMN OF PRAISE

> *The heavens are telling the glory of God;*
> *and the firmament proclaims his handiwork.*
> *Day to day pours forth speech,*
> *and night to night declares knowledge.*

Here, as Weiser says, the Psalmist 'contemplates with awe the majesty of God revealed in creation'. The Psalm is 'the fruit of the rapture which was aroused in him by the moving experience of God in Nature'. Ewald, one of the older commentators, writes: 'The heaven (the sky), as one of the divine works, becomes for every man who is not utterly insensible, the most eloquent witness and most speaking herald of the glory of its Master and Creator in all his works.' Nature itself, says Weiser, is 'the record of creation, an essential part of the self-revelation of God to the whole world'.

The *heavens*, of course, are the sky, ruled by the sun by day and scattered with the stars at night. The creation of the *firmament* is related in the creation story. The RSV has it:

And God said, Let there be a firmament in the midst of the waters, and let it separate the waters from the waters. And God made the firmament and separated the waters which were under the firmament from the waters which were above the firmament. And it was so. And God called the firmament Heaven

(Genesis 1.7-8)

The still newer translations make the picture clearer; the NEB has:

God said, Let there be a vault between the waters, to separate water from water. So God made the vault, and separated the water under the vault from the water above it, and so it was; and God called the vault heaven.

The early creation stories are told with a childlike simplicity. The sky was regarded as a vast, solid, transparent dome, built over the earth like a great plate. Omar Khayyam speaks of 'that inverted bowl we call the sky'. And the blue of the sky was the blue of the waters of heaven seen through the transparent dome, which was the firmament.

So to the Psalmist the sky by day and by night declares the glory of God. The days and the nights keep up a kind of endless chain of ceaseless praise. As A. F. Kirkpatrick puts it: 'Each day, each night, hands on the message to its successor in an unbroken tradition.' So Eaton speaks of 'the ceaseless testimony which fills the cosmos'. Nature is for ever raising its *Te Deum* to God.

This personification of nature is characteristic of the poetry of the Bible.

> The heavens declare his righteousness,
>   for God himself is judge!
>
> (Psalm 50.6)

> The heavens proclaim his righteousness;
>   and all the peoples behold his glory
>
> (Psalm 97.6)

Psalm 148 is one of the great praising Psalms and summons the whole universe to the glorification of God.

> Praise the Lord!
> Praise the Lord from the heavens,
>   praise him in the heights!
> Praise him, all his angels,
>   praise him, all his host!
>
> Praise him, sun and moon,
>   praise him, all you shining stars!
> Praise him, you highest heavens,
>   and you waters above the heavens!

Praise the Lord from the earth,
    you sea monsters and all deeps,
fire and hail, snow and frost,
    stormy wind fulfilling his command!

Mountains and all hills,
    fruit trees and all cedars!
Beasts and all cattle,
    creeping things and flying birds!

(1-4; 7-10)

The most tremendous of all the nature hymns is The Song of the
Three Young Men, which is one of the additions to Daniel in the
Apocrypha:

Bless the Lord, all works of the Lord,
    sing praise to him and highly exalt him for ever.
Bless the Lord, you heavens,
    sing praise to him and highly exalt him for ever.
Bless the Lord, you angels of the Lord,
    sing praise to him and highly exalt him for ever.
Bless the Lord, all waters above the heaven,
    sing praise to him and highly exalt him for ever.
Bless the Lord, all powers,
    sing praise to him and highly exalt him for ever.
Bless the Lord, sun and moon,
    sing praise to him and highly exalt him for ever.
Bless the Lord, stars of heaven,
    sing praise to him and highly exalt him for ever.
Bless the Lord, all rain and dew,
    sing praise to him and highly exalt him for ever.
Bless the Lord, all winds,
    sing praise to him and highly exalt him for ever.

Bless the Lord, fire and heat,
  sing praise to him and highly exalt him for ever.
Bless the Lord, winter cold and summer heat,
  sing praise to him and highly exalt him for ever.
Bless the Lord, dews and snows,
  sing praise to him and highly exalt him for ever.
Bless the Lord, nights and days,
  sing praise to him and highly exalt him for ever.
Bless the Lord, light and darkness,
  sing praise to him and highly exalt him for ever.
Bless the Lord, ice and cold,
  sing praise to him and highly exalt him for ever.
Bless the Lord, frosts and snows,
  sing praise to him and highly exalt him for ever.
Bless the Lord, lightnings and clouds,
  sing praise to him and highly exalt him for ever.
Let the earth bless the Lord;
  let it sing praise to him and highly exalt him for ever.
Bless the Lord, mountains and hills,
  sing praise to him and highly exalt him for ever.
Bless the Lord, all things that grow on the earth,
  sing praise to him and highly exalt him for ever.
Bless the Lord, you springs,
  sing praise to him and highly exalt him for ever.
Bless the Lord, seas and rivers,
  sing praise to him and highly exalt him for ever.
Bless the Lord, you whales and all creatures that move in the
    waters,
  sing praise to him and highly exalt him for ever.
Bless the Lord, all birds of the air,
  sing praise to him and highly exalt him for ever.
Bless the Lord, all beasts and cattle,
  sing praise to him and highly exalt him for ever

                        (The Song of the Three Young Men 35-39)

There is the same chorus of praise in St Francis's hymn:

> All creatures of our God and King,
> Lift up your voice and with us sing
>   Alleluia, Alleluia!
> Thou burning sun with golden beam,
> Thou silver moon with softer gleam,
>   O praise him, O praise him,
>   Alleluia, Alleluia, Alleluia!
>
> Thou rushing wind that art so strong,
> Ye clouds that sail in heaven along,
>   O praise him, Alleluia!
> Thou rising morn, in praise rejoice,
> Ye lights of evening find a voice.
>
> Thou flowing water, pure and clear,
> Make music for thy Lord to hear,
>   Alleluia, Alleluia!
> Thou fire so masterful and bright,
> That givest man both warmth and light.
>
> Dear mother earth, who day by day
> Unfoldest blessings on our way,
>   O praise him, Alleluia!
> The flowers and fruits that in thee grow,
> Let them his glory also show.

For those who have eyes to see and ears to hear, nature is for ever praising God. No Christian could ever sing: 'Earth is a desert drear.'

Verse 3, 4b　ELOQUENCE WITHOUT WORDS

> *There is no speech, nor are there words;*
> *their voice is not heard;*
> *yet their voice goes out through all the earth,*
> *and their words to the end of the world.*

Here the modern translations correct the AV which runs:

> There is no speech nor language,
> where their voice is not heard.
> Their line is gone out through all the earth,
> and their words to the end of the world.

The point is not that words and speech have gone out to the end of the earth but that, although in nature there are no words, there is an eloquent silence in which God makes himself known. The Jerusalem Bible has:

> No utterance at all, no speech,
> no sound that anyone can hear;
> yet their voice goes out through all the earth,
> and their message to the ends of the world.

There is a further point of meaning to note. In the RSV in verse 3 we have: 'Their *voice* is not heard.' In verse 4 we have: 'Yet their *voice* goes out through all the earth.' The Hebrew word for *voice* in verse 3 is not the same as that in verse 4. The Jerusalem Bible, to make the differentiation, uses *voice* in the first instance and *message* in the second; but in the second instance the meaning of the word is rather *sound, reverberation*, and the New English Bible brings this out:

> And this without speech or language
> or sound of any voice.
> Their *music* goes out through all the earth,
> their words reach to the end of the world.

From nature comes a voice without words, a revelation of God
which is beyond speech, a kind of music which is an echo of his
voice.

Weiser speaks of this self-revelation of God in nature. 'The
language which God speaks through nature is not tied to the
linguistic frontiers of men . . . There is no language in which
that silent voice of God's revelation in nature would not make
itself heard and understood.' 'The language of nature is
understood in every part of the world . . . The heavens are the
book from which the whole world can derive its knowledge of
God.' Approached with reverence, nature gives a 'glimpse into
the interior of God's workshop'. He who has never read a book
in his life can see God in the world which God's hand has made.

Two poets have specially laid hold on this thought of God in
nature. Addison made a kind of expanded paraphrase of this
very Psalm:

> The spacious firmament on high,
> With all the blue ethereal sky,
> And spangled heavens, a shining frame,
> Their great Original proclaim.
> The unwearied sun, from day to day,
> Does his Creator's power display,
> And publishes to every land
> The work of an Almighty hand.
>
> Soon as the evening shades prevail,
> The moon takes up the wondrous tale,
> And nightly to the listening earth
> Repeats the story of her birth;
> While all the stars that round her burn,
> And all the planets, in their turn,
> Confirm the tidings, as they roll,
> And spread the truth from pole to pole.

What though in solemn silence all
Move round the dark terrestrial ball?
What though no real voice or sound
Amidst their radiant orbs be found?
In reason's ear they all rejoice,
And utter forth a glorious voice,
For ever singing as they shine,
'The hand that made us is divine.'

Nature is a silent but eloquent witness to God, a witness which needs no translator.

The other poet is Wordsworth, especially in the poem written near Tintern Abbey. He tells how his experience of nature had two stages. At first he was thrilled and fascinated by the sheer, physical, sensuous beauty of nature.

For Nature then
To me was all in all. I cannot paint
What then I was. The sounding cataract
Haunted me like a passion; the tall rock,
The mountain, and the deep and gloomy wood,
Their colors and their forms were then to me
An appetite; a feeling and a love,
That had no need of a remoter charm,
By thought supplied, or any interest
Unborrow'd from the eye.

At that stage the very sight of nature moved him to the depths of his being. Then came the second stage, when he began to find in nature something beyond itself, something more deeply moving than the surface beauty.

> And I have felt
> A presence that disturbs me with the joy
> Of elevated thoughts; a sense sublime
> Of something far more deeply interfused,
> Whose dwelling is the light of setting suns,
> And the round ocean, and the living air,
> And the blue sky, and in the mind of man;
> A motion and a spirit, that impels
> All thinking things, all objects of all thought,
> And rolls through all things.

It was no longer simply a sensuous, physical beauty Wordsworth found in nature; it was God.

It is true that nature can be red in tooth and claw; it is true that man's pollution can defile nature; but God is there. Millais, the famous artist, tells how he came to see nature. His father, an old countryman, would take him out towards evening, and they would lie beside the cornfield and watch the rabbits play and the corn sway like a wave of the sea beneath the breeze. One evening, as there came upon the world a sunset of unutterable beauty, the old man rose, faced the splendor of the dying sun, took off his cap, and said softly: 'My son, it is God.' There would be no more pollution and no more destruction and no more desecration, if men would learn to reverence not only God, but also his handiwork.

Carlyle wrote: 'He who in any way shows us better than we knew before that a lily of the fields is beautiful, does he not show it us as an effluence of the Fountain of all Beauty; as the *handwriting*, made visible there, of the great Maker of the Universe? He has sung for us, made us sing with him, "a little verse of a sacred Psalm".'

Verses 4b-6   THE SAFETY OF CERTAINTY

In them he has set a tent for the sun,
which comes forth like a bridegroom leaving his chamber,
   and like a strong man runs its course with joy.
Its rising is from the end of the heavens,
   and its circuit to the end of them;
   and there is nothing hid from its heat.

From one point of view there is nothing unusual about this passage. The sun is often connected with God. When the day of the Lord comes, 'for you who fear my name the sun of righteousness shall rise, with healing in its wings' (Malachi 4.2). The prayer for the king is:

> May his name endure for ever,
>   his fame continue as long as the sun!

> (Psalm 72.17)

The promise to David is:

> His line shall endure for ever,
>   his throne as long as the sun before me

> (Psalm 89.36)

God's justice is to go forth 'for a light to the peoples' (Isaiah 51.4).

In Moses' last blessing of the people, he says:

> The Lord came from Sinai,
>   and dawned from Seir upon us;
>   he shone forth from Mount Paran

> (Deuteronomy 33.2)

There was nothing unusual in seeing in the sun the symbol of that which lasts for ever.

What is unusual is that the Psalmist takes a pagan myth and

uses it for his own purposes. Of course, the ancient peoples believed that it was the sun which moved, not the earth, and the science of the biblical writers was the science of their day. There was an ancient myth which said that, when the sun had made his daily journey across the sky, he was weary and at the end of the world there was a tent where he spent the night in the arms of Ocean his mistress to rise refreshed in the morning to make his journey again.

The RSV has the picture of the sun leaving his chamber like a bridegroom to make his daily journey. The NEB more correctly speaks of the sun coming out like a bridegroom from his wedding canopy. The word for *canopy* is *huppah* and it means the ritual canopy under which a bride and bridegroom were married. This is pure mythology; the Psalmist is taking a heathen myth and fearlessly using it for his own purposes. Heathen poetry though it is, the Psalmist appropriates its beauty.

Here is something of which Christianity has been too often shrinkingly afraid. Too often the Church has been afraid to use the loveliness which is in the pagan world. Once a lady complained to that great scholar and mystic, von Hügel, that it was wrong to turn to Homer and Pindar from Tertullian and Augustine. He wrote to her:

> If there is one danger for religion, if there is any one plausible,
> all but irresistible trend, which throughout its long rich history
> has sapped its force and prepared the most destructive counter
> excesses, it is just that – that allowing of the fascination of grace
> to deaden and ignore the beauties and duties of nature.

If we are really sure of our faith we will not be afraid of the loveliness of the world. The Psalmist has no fear of taking and using a lovely heathen story.

No one would question the sincerity of the Puritans, but they were extraordinarily terrified of the beauty of the world. John Richard Green in the *Short History of the English People* writes: 'Little things became great things in the glare of religious zeal; and the godly man learned to shrink from a surplice, or a mincepie at Christmas, as he shrank from the impurity of a lie. Life became hard, rigid, and colorless as it became intense. The play, the geniality, the delight of the Elizabethan age were exchanged for a measured sobriety, seriousness and self-restraint'.

The feeling was that beauty and joy were dangerous. Macaulay in his *History of England* describes the same period. The Prayer Book was a thing of the devil. 'It was a crime in a child to read by the bedside of a sick parent one of those beautiful collects which had soothed the griefs of forty generations of Christians.' Beautiful churches and works of art were shattered with the hammer. Any pictures of Jesus and of the Virgin Mother were sentenced to be destroyed. Public shows were violently attacked. Theatres were closed and dismantled, and the actors whipped through the streets at the cart's tail. Maypoles were hewn down.

This was a fear of beauty and of joy from which the Psalmist was totally liberated. God, said the writer of the Pastoral Epistles, 'richly furnishes us with everything to enjoy' (I Timothy 6.17). The Rabbis had a saying that a man will give account for every good thing he might have enjoyed and did not.

Once a man has the utter certainty of the Psalmist he need have no fear of the beauty the world offers him.

The section finishes with a very human touch. Nothing is hidden from the sun's heat. Here, says W. E. Barnes, speaks the Eastern, cowering in the black tent of skin and gasping because of the heat.

Verses 7-9 THE JOY OF THE LAW

The law of the Lord is perfect,
  reviving the soul;
the testimony of the Lord is sure,
  making wise the simple;
the precepts of the Lord are right,
  rejoicing the heart;
the commandment of the Lord is pure,
  enlightening the eyes;
the fear of the Lord is clean,
  enduring for ever;
the ordinances of the Lord are true,
  and righteous altogether.

The Psalmist has spoken of the wonder of nature and now he goes on to sing the praises of the law. In the passage with which we are now dealing the Psalmist uses Jahweh no fewer than six times and it is significant that in this second part of the Psalm he should change the name he uses for God. In verse 1 he uses El, which means the Powerful One and is a name that could be used for a god of any religion; but when he comes to speak of the law he uses Jahweh, for Jahweh is not anyone's god but Israel's God, the God who entered into covenant relationship with her and gave her the law.

In the three verses of the Psalm which we are now considering, the Psalmist uses six different words to describe the law, six different descriptions of it and six different effects which it has.

The *law* is *perfect* and *revives the soul*. He begins with the widest word. The *law* is God's teaching in all its fullness. God, as it has been said, has taken the trouble to make himself known to men and the law is his self-revelation. It is not simply a matter of a collection of rules and regulations, however important. In the law there is history and event, for God reveals himself in action as well as in word.

That law is *perfect*. The word is *tamim*. It is used to describe a sacrifice without spot or blemish and fit to offer to God. It is used to describe the work of God. 'The Rock, his work is perfect' (Deuteronomy 32.4). It is used to describe the knowledge of God (Job 37.16). It is used to describe the way of life which God's People ought to live (Deuteronomy 18.13). The law then, as the Psalmist sees it, is the complete revelation of the will of God, beyond which nothing more is necessary.

It *revives* the soul. An even better translation is that it *refreshes* the soul. 'New life for the soul', as the Jerusalem Bible translates it. The law, as W. E. Barnes says, is 'a moral tonic'. God's law is not something negative and frustrating and depressing; it is the revelation of the full life God wants us to live, and the guidance and the inspiration to live it.

The *testimony* of the Lord is *sure, making wise the simple*. The two tablets of the law, given to Moses on Sinai, are regularly called the tablets of testimony.

> And he gave to Moses, when he had made an end of speaking with him upon Mount Sinai, the two tables of the testimony, tables of stone, written with the finger of God
>
> (Exodus 31.18)

> And Moses turned, and went down from the mountain with the two tables of the testimony in his hands, tables that were written on both sides; on the one side and on the other were they written. And the tables were the work of God, and the writing was the writing of God, graven upon the tables
>
> (Exodus 32.15)

This testimony was put into the ark and lodged in the Holy of Holies (Exodus 25.16, 21; 27.21); and the ark became known as the ark of the testimony (Exodus 31.7). The law is God's testimony to himself, for in it there is the manifestation of his will, and there is the very foundation on which the covenant, the relationship between God and Israel, depends. And the law is God's testimony to man, for it lays down his will for man and man's duty to God and to his fellow men.

That testimony is *sure*. There are three possible ideas behind the word – the law never fails, the law is absolutely trustworthy, the law is completely stable in a world in which so much is liable to change and decay.

This law, as the Jerusalem Bible translates it, is 'wisdom for the simple'. The word *simple* is a favorite word in Proverbs, *pethi*. It does not mean simple intellectually; it is rather what we might call a simpleton. John Paterson describes the character of the *pethi* in *The Book that is Alive*. He is basically open and accessible. 'It all depends who gets him first.' He is 'open to the solicitations of Madame Folly', but also to the appeal of the Sage. He is full of possibilities for prudence and folly; he is the raw material on which the Sage can work. The Proverbs are written 'that prudence may be given to the simple' (Proverbs 1.4). 'How long, O simple ones, will you love being simple? How long will scoffers delight in their scoffing, and fools hate knowledge?' (Proverbs 1.22).

> A prudent man sees danger and hides himself,
>> but the simple go on and suffer for it
>>> (Proverbs 22.3)

> The simple believes everything,
>> but the prudent looks where he is going
>>> (Proverbs 14.15)

The law of the Lord is such that even the simpleton can live well if he will take it as the guide and director of his life.

Obedience to the law brings safety to the simple.

The *precepts* of the Lord are *right, rejoicing the heart.*
Precepts are various special injunctions about particular things;
the AV sometimes calls them *statutes.* They are *right*; there are
two ideas here – that of *correctness* and that of *directness.* They
give the right information and they give it with a directness
which brooks no mistake. The precepts *rejoice the heart* – 'joy
for the heart', as the Jerusalem Bible translates it. In the El
Amarna tablets a worshipper says: 'When I heard the words on
the tablet of the King, my Lord, my heart rejoiced and my eyes
became very radiant.' It is to be noted that in Hebrew the heart
is not so much the seat of the emotions as it is in English; the
heart is the seat of the intellect and the will. So we may say that
in the precepts of the law a man may find joy for his heart and
satisfaction for his intellect.

The *commandment* of the Lord is *pure, enlightening the eyes.*
The *commandment* is a general instruction for life from God.
For *pure* the NEB has *shines clear*; the commandment is clear
and radiant – 'light to the eyes', as the Jerusalem Bible translates
it. The Proverbs have it:

> The commandment is a lamp and the teaching a light
>
> (Proverbs 6.23)

The commandment of the Lord is like a lamp to light a dark
pathway.

The *fear* of the Lord is *clean, enduring for ever. Fear* is the
one word that seems out of place with the other five – law,
testimony, precepts, commandment, ordinances – and it has
been suggested that it should be *edict.* But the change is not
necessary. *Fear* of the Lord means *reverence* for the Lord; it is
not fear in the sense of being afraid, but in the sense of respect
and awe. That fear is *clean* or, maybe better, *pure.* It is pure in

the sense that refined metal is pure with no dross in it. The point is that in the other religions there were elements of impurity. For instance, the worshippers of Molech burned their children in the fire as offerings to their god (Leviticus 18.21; II Kings 23.10). In the shrines of the Baals, the Canaanite gods, many of the priestesses were sacred prostitutes. There were blots on the other religions but the worship of Jahweh was pure.

The *ordinances* of the Lord are *true*, and *righteous altogether*. The ordinances are the decrees, the decisions, the judgments of God; they are true and all are *righteous*. God's decisions are given in truth and preserve the truth.

Such then is the loving tribute of the Psalmist to the law. Let us hear it once again, this time in the neat translation of the Jerusalem Bible:

> The Law of Jahweh is perfect,
>   new life for the soul;
> the decree of Jahweh is trustworthy,
>   wisdom for the simple.
>
> The precepts of Jahweh are upright,
>   joy for the heart;
> the commandment of Jahweh is clear,
>   light for the eyes.
>
> The fear of the Lord is pure,
>   lasting for ever;
> the judgments of the Lord are true,
>   righteous, every one.

For the Psalmist, as it has been well said, 'the law is the point at which an encounter takes place with the living God, who reveals himself in the law'.

Verses 10, 11   THE ULTIMATE REWARD

More to be desired are they than gold,
    even much fine gold;
sweeter also than honey
    and drippings of the honeycomb.

Moreover by them is thy servant warned;
    in keeping them there is great reward.

The teachings of the law are more precious than fine gold.

It is said that when a little Jewish boy was learning the alphabet, his teacher sometimes offered him a reward. The letters of the alphabet were written on a slate; and they were written, not with chalk or with slate-pencil, but in a mixture of flour and honey. The teacher would point at a letter and ask what it was and, if the boy could answer correctly, he was allowed to lick the letter off the slate! Learning for him was as sweet as honey. Learning the law was sweeter than honey and more precious than gold.

The Psalmist looked forward to his reward if he faithfully kept the law. Nowadays we are very suspicious of introducing the reward motive. It is told of an old saint that he said that he would like to obliterate the joys of Paradise and extinguish the flames of hell so that people might obey God simply for the sake of obeying and not for the sake of any reward. But the Bible is never afraid of the reward motive. Jesus said:

> Truly, I say unto you, whoever gives you a cup of water to drink because you bear the name of Christ, will by no means lose his reward
>
> (Mark 9.41)

> Blessed are you when men hate you, and when they exclude you and revile you, and cast out your name as evil, on account of

the Son of Man! Rejoice in that day, and leap for joy, for behold, your reward is great in heaven; for so their fathers did to the prophets

(Luke 6.22, 23)

If you do good to those who do good to you, what credit is that to you? For even sinners do the same. And if you lend to those from whom you hope to receive, what credit is that to you? Even sinners lend to sinners, to receive as much again. But love your enemies, and do good, and lend, expecting nothing in return; and your reward will be great, and you will be sons of the Most High

(Luke 6.33-35)

Paul said:

for he will render to every man according to his works; to those who by patience in well-doing seek for glory and honor and immortality, he will give eternal life; but for those who are factious and do not obey the truth, but obey wickedness, there will be wrath and fury. There will be tribulation and distress for every human being who does evil, the Jew first and also the Greek, but glory and honor and peace for everyone who does good, the Jew first and also the Greek. For God shows no partiality

(Romans 2.6-11)

The Bible does not shirk the reward motive, and why should it? Unless a thing is good for something, it is good for nothing. But what is the reward which the Psalmist expects and will receive? Different interpreters have made different suggestions.

i. There is the reward of the experience which comes to a man from the enjoyment of the law. The man who in discipline, devotion and dedication lives well has a joy that slack living can never bring.

ii. There is the reward which comes in ever new strength, new joy, new wisdom, new enlightenment. The reward of hard study is the ability to move on to higher and harder study; the reward of diligent training is the ability acquired to move on to greater demands. To keep the law is ever to be moving to new horizons both of understanding and performance; it is a life which is on the way.

iii. There is the reward of the relief which comes from being protected from taking the wrong way. To know the right way is at least the first step to taking it. The law makes possible right decisions for the man who knows it and is determined to keep it.

iv. There is the reward of a clear conscience. As Dickens pointed out long ago, once you do a wrong thing, the whole world becomes your enemy. Epicurus believed that pleasure was the highest good, but he believed that pleasure and virtue go hand in hand, and that the evil-doer could never be happy, for, apart from anything else, there is the constant fear of being found out.

v. There is the inner freedom which obedience brings. When a man has habituated himself to obedience to God and conscience, so far from living a more confined life, he has entered into a freedom from the passions and the instincts which he well knows can ruin life.

vi. All these are fine rewards. But there is no doubt that the Hebrew would expect material rewards as well.

> The reward for humility and fear of the Lord
>   is riches and honor and life

(Proverbs 22.4)

At least in the early days the Hebrew thinker had no real belief in any life after death and therefore he expected his rewards in the here and now. We have learned not to expect that goodness will bring material reward but beyond a doubt it brings its reward in a happiness, a satisfaction, and a peace of mind that nothing else can bring.

Verses 12, 13   LIFE AT RISK

But who can discern his errors?
   Clear thou me from hidden faults.
Keep back thy servant also from presumptuous sins;
   let them not have dominion over me!
Then I shall be blameless,
   and innocent of great transgression.

It is one thing to know the right thing to do; it is entirely another to do it. The Psalmist has sung his lyric praise of the law and now he prays to God that he may keep him from breaking the law which he knows and loves.

John Drinkwater wrote a famous poem in which he says that we do not pray for light in darkness, for the lifted veil, for the clearer vision, for the fuller knowledge. All these things we have:

Not these. We know the hemlock from the rose,
The pure from stained, the noble from the base,
The tranquil holy light that glows
   On Pity's face.

We know the paths wherein our feet should press,
Across our hearts are written Thy decrees.
Yet now, O Lord, be merciful to bless
   With more than these.

> Grant us the will to fashion as we feel,
> Grant us the strength to labor as we know,
> Grant us the purpose, ribbed and edged with steel,
>   To strike the blow.
>
> Knowledge we ask not – knowledge Thou hast lent;
> But, Lord, the will – there lies our deepest need.
> Grant us to build above the high intent
>   The deed, the deed.

That is precisely the frame of mind of the Psalmist. He knows the law; he loves the law; how can he live the law? So he asks God to keep him from three things.

i. He asks to be kept from *errors*. Errors are sins of ignorance or inadvertence. They are committed when a man is off his guard or when he does not know any better. There is nothing deliberate about sins like that. The Jewish law made provision for atonement for what it calls sinning *unwittingly* (Leviticus 4.2, 13; Numbers 15.22-26). The sin which is done without deliberation, whether it is done in ignorance, through inadvertence, unwittingly or in a moment's passion, was for the Hebrew a forgivable sin.

ii. He asks to be kept from *hidden faults* or, as the NEB puts it, the secret fault. This is not so much the fault which a man tries to keep secret from other people, or the fault which he tries to keep secret from himself by refusing to look at it, or the fault which with the supreme folly a man may try to keep secret from God. This is rather the fault of which a man is not conscious. So the Psalmist prays to be kept from the sins of which he is not even aware – and so must we all.

iii. The RSV and nearly all the translations then depict the Psalmist as praying to be kept from *presumptuous sins*; and this

may well be the right translation. The sin committed
deliberately, in defiance of the known will of God, was the most
serious of all. The Old Testament law in a vivid phrase calls it
the sin of 'the high hand'.

> The person who does anything with a high hand, whether he is
> native or a sojourner, reviles the Lord, and that person shall be
> cut off from among his people. Because he has despised the
> word of the Lord, and has broken his commandment, that
> person shall be utterly cut off; his iniquity shall be upon him
>
> (Numbers 15.30, 31)

This is the sin of supreme pride, the sin of the man who
deliberately sets his own will above the will of God. There is
forgiveness for the man who has accidentally killed another,
even if that be done in passion, but,

> If a man willfully attacks another to kill him treacherously, you
> shall take him from my altar that he may die
>
> (Exodus 21.12-14)

(The man who accidentally killed another was entitled to take
refuge at the altar). It is the same for the man who in his pride
will not accept the verdict of the priest or judge:

> The man who acts presumptuously, by not obeying the priest
> who stands to minister there before the Lord your God, or the
> judge, that man shall die; so you shall purge the evil from Israel.
> And all the people shall hear, and fear, and not act
> presumptuously again
>
> (Deuteronomy 17.12, 13)

So then it may be – it may even be probable – that the
Psalmist is praying that he may never fall into the deliberate sin
which prefers its own will to the will of God.

iv. There is another very interesting possibility. The Psalmist prays to be delivered from *zedim*. Elsewhere *zedim* are not presumptuous sins but presumptuous men. They are men who themselves have arrogantly abandoned God, and who encourage, and even force, others to do the same. They appear characteristically in Psalm 119, as a constant threat to the godly man, and they are in the RSV translated *the godless*; in the NEB they are *proud men*.

> Godless men utterly deride me,
>   but I do not turn away from thy law
>
> (Psalm 119.51)

> The godless besmear me with lies,
>   but with my whole heart I keep thy precepts
>
> (Psalm 119.69)

> Let the godless be put to shame,
>   because they have subverted me with guile;
>   as for me, I will meditate on thy precepts
>
> (Psalm 119.78)

> Godless men have dug pitfalls for me,
>   men who do not conform to thy law
>
> (Psalm 119.85)

> Be surety for thy servant for good;
>   let not the godless oppress me
>
> (Psalm 119.122)

Let them not have dominion over me, says the Psalmist; and it may be that he is praying for strength to resist the pressure of those who have lost their own faith in God and are out to destroy the faith of everyone else. The Christian has to be prepared to resist the militant propaganda of those who are anti-God. 'Let them not have dominion over me!'

Verse 14 THE SACRIFICE AND THE SAVIOR

Let the words of my mouth and the meditation of
my heart be acceptable in thy sight,
O Lord, my rock and my redeemer.

The Psalmist asks that his words and his thoughts may be acceptable to God. He uses the same word as a worshipper used when he asked God *to accept* the sacrifice he brought to the altar. The law lays down just what kind of offering a man must bring 'that he may be accepted before the Lord' (Leviticus 1.3, 4). This means that the Psalmist wishes to offer his words and his thoughts as a sacrifice to God. This is a thought that occurs more than once in the Psalms:

> I will praise the name of God with a song;
>   I will magnify him with thanksgiving.
> This will please the Lord more than an ox
>   or a bull with horns and hoofs
>
> (Psalm 69.30, 31)

The Psalmist has arrived at the stage where he can believe that the sacrifice of the loving heart is dearer to God than the sacrifice of any animal.

> Let my prayer be counted as incense before thee,
>   and the lifting up of my hands as an evening sacrifice!
>
> (Psalm 141.2)

> Accept my offerings of praise, O Lord,
>   and teach me thy ordinances
>
> (Psalm 119.108)

It is the Psalmist of the 19th Psalm who has the greatest vision. It is not so difficult to think of prayer and praise as an offering to God; but the writer of this 19th Psalm wishes so to live that his every thought is pure enough and his every word clean enough to be an unblemished offering to God.

Then he goes on to call God by two names. First he calls him *my Rock*. This is a common name for God, so much so that Rock is very nearly the equivalent of God. For the Psalmist God is 'my Rock' (18.46; 28.1). In a strange phrase God is 'the rock that begat you' (Deuteronomy 32.18). When comparing God and the triumphs of God with the gods of the other nations, Moses can say: 'Their rock is not as our rock' (Deuteronomy 32.31). David in his triumph song asks: 'Who is a rock, except our God?' (II Samuel 22.32). Isaiah hears God say: 'Is there a God besides me? There is no Rock; I know not any' (Isaiah 44.8). Habakkuk can actually use the word as we would use a proper name:

> O Lord, thou hast ordained them as a judgment;
>   and thou, O Rock, hast established them for
>   chastisement
>
> (Habakkuk 1.12)

To the idea of the Rock certain ideas characteristically cling. Again and again the Rock is a rock of refuge (Deuteronomy 32.37; II Samuel 22.3; Psalm 31.2; 62.7; Isaiah 17.10).

> The Lord has become my stronghold,
>   and my God the Rock of my refuge
>
> (Psalm 94.22)

Again and again the Rock is the rock of salvation (Psalm 89.26; 95.1).

> He only is my Rock and my salvation,
>   my fortress; I shall not be shaken
>
> (Psalm 62.6)

God is the everlasting Rock:

> Trust in the Lord for ever,
>> for the Lord God is an everlasting Rock
>
> (Isaiah 26.4)

To call God the Rock is to call him the Protector, the one in whose shadow there is rest from the dust and heat of the day, the one in whose clefts there is refuge from danger. To call God the Rock is to think of his solidity and permanence in a world in which so much is shifting sand.

There is sheer loveliness in the word *redeemer*. In this case the word has not as its main idea that of ransom from captivity or the like, as is the case when it is used of God redeeming Israel from bondage in Egypt. The word is *goēl*. The *goēl* was the nearest relative. It was his duty to help and protect his kinsman in any time of difficulty or of danger, to ransom him from slavery should he become a slave, to avenge his death should he be murdered, to take upon himself the responsibility for his wife and family should he die. The *goēl* was the nearest relative to whom the life and welfare of his kinsman were as dear as his own. So the Psalm closes with the same great word that Job used, when he said: 'I know that my Redeemer lives' (Job 19.25). It closes with the affirmation that God is the kinsman of every man and that he cares.

NATURE AND LAW

So this Psalm brings back to our memories two things which nowadays we are apt to forget.

i. The wonder with which the Psalmist regards the world reminds us that there is such a thing as Natural Theology. In the older days a distinction used to be drawn between two kinds of theology. There was Natural Theology which was based on what could be learned about God from the world. Natural

Theology was therefore open to every man, for nature is a book which all may read. The other kind of theology was Revealed Theology. This was based on the special revelation which God gave in the Bible and in Jesus Christ. Revealed Theology therefore was something which belonged to the Christian and to the outsider was a closed book. Less and less stress came to be laid on Natural Theology and more and more stress on Revealed Theology until a stage was reached when it was held that there was no true way of learning about God except from God's book and God's Son. This Psalm takes us back to the truth that in God's world we can see God. As J. Y. Simpson used to put it, the world is the garment of the living God. Tertullian often argued from the world to God. He writes to Marcion who believed that this was an evil world created by an evil God: 'One flower of the hedge-row by itself, I think – I do not say a flower of the meadows; one shell of any sea you like – I do not say the Red Sea; one feather of a moorfowl – to say nothing of a peacock – will they speak to you of a mean Creator?' 'Copy if you can the buildings of the bee, the barns of the ant, the web of the spider.' 'If I offer you a rose, you will not scorn its Creator.' To Tertullian the world was the proof of the skill, the power and the love of God.

Long before Tertullian, Aristotle had imagined what would happen if people who had been kept all their lives captive below the earth were suddenly released and confronted with nature. What would their reaction be? It is Cicero who quotes the passage (*On the Nature of the Gods* 2.37.95):

> If there were beings who had always lived beneath the earth, in comfortable, well-lit dwellings, decorated with statues and pictures and furnished with all the luxuries enjoyed by persons thought to be supremely happy, and who though they had never come forth above the ground had learned by report and by

hearsay of the existence of certain deities or divine powers; and then if at some time the jaws of the earth were opened and they were able to escape from their hidden abode and to come forth into the regions we inhabit; when they suddenly had sight of the earth and the seas and the sky, and came to know of the vast clouds and mighty winds, and beheld the sun, and realized not only its size and beauty but also its potency in causing the day by shedding light over all the sky, and after night had darkened the earth, they saw the whole sky spangled and adorned with stars, and the changing phases of the moon's light, now waxing and now waning, and the risings and settings of all these heavenly bodies and their courses fixed and changeless throughout all eternity – when they saw these things, surely they would think that the gods exist and that these mighty marvels are their handiwork.

If you saw a splendid house, Cicero says, you surely would not assume that it was built by mice or weasels. A splendid house implies a splendid architect; and a wonderful world implies a divine creator.

There is still a place for Natural Theology, for arguing from the here and now to the there and then, for arguing from the seen to the unseen, for arguing from the world to God.

ii. The second half-forgotten truth with which this Psalm confronts us is the greatness of law. Law is an unpopular concept nowadays; freedom has taken its place. But it must never be forgotten that the Psalmist speaks with sheer delight of the law. For him the law was no grim yoke; it was the greatest thing in the world. The law, says Weiser, was given to men to educate and to save them. In the law is embodied the mutual relationship between God and man. The law, says Kirkpatrick, quickens and educates man's moral nature. There are certain things to be said about the law and certain values to be recognized.

The law provides a man with a chart of the way of life. The law says: 'This is the way you must live, this is the path you must walk if you wish to reach your real journey's end.' The law gives a man a touchstone by which he may test courses of action. The law enables a man to make decisions. All these things are valuable. But the tendency has been to stress freedom, to play down discipline, to recommend a policy of 'do as you like'.

It is very significant that that position is being put into reverse even by some who held it most strongly. In America the great apostle of freedom was Dr Benjamin Spock, freedom from all conventions, freedom from all moral demands, freedom to 'express yourself'. But here are two passages which Dr Benjamin Spock has more recently written:

> For decades I was an uncompromising civil libertarian, and scorned the hypocrisy involved in the enforcement of obscenity laws, but recent trends in movies, literature and art towards that which I think of as shock obscenity, and the courts' acceptance of it, have made me change my position . . . particularly in view of other brutalizing trends . . . In our so-called emancipation from our Puritan past I think we've lost our bearings. Many enlightened parents still have inner convictions but are afraid that they don't have a sure basis for teaching them to their children. Some of their children are quite bewildered, as child psychiatrists and school counselors report.

A generation without law is a generation adrift, as even the anti-law people have come to see. The second passage from Dr Spock runs like this:

> Recently I've come to realize that the worst problems of America . . . are caused not by lack of knowledge or means but by moral blindness or confusion . . . Many youths are left in a vacuum. They are offered no set of values either to subscribe to

or to argue about. This situation amounts to a serious deficiency disease for a species designed to live by the spirit.

The clear conclusion is that though the Christian must live by grace he cannot dispense with law, a law which must be his guide and not his chain.

Psalm 104

GOD'S WORLD

Bless the LORD, O my soul!
   O LORD my god, thou art very great!
2 Thou art clothed with honor and majesty,
    who coverest thyself with light as with a garment,
  who hast stretched out the heavens like a tent,
3   who hast laid the beams of thy chambers on the waters,
  who makest the clouds thy chariot,
    who ridest on the wings of the wind,
4 who makest the winds thy messengers,
   fire and flame thy ministers.

5 Thou didst set the earth on its foundations,
   so that it should never be shaken.
6 Thou didst cover it with the deep as with a garment;
   the waters stood above the mountains.
7 At thy rebuke they fled;
   at the sound of thy thunder they took to flight.
8 The mountains rose, the valleys sank down
   to the place which thou didst appoint for them.
9 Thou didst set a bound which they should not pass,
   so that they might not again cover the earth.

10 Thou makest springs gush forth in the valleys;
   they flow between the hills,
11 they give drink to every beast of the field;
   the wild asses quench their thirst.
12 By them the birds of the air have their habitation;

they sing among the branches.

¹³ From thy lofty abode thou waterest the mountains;
the earth is satisfied with the fruit of thy work.

¹⁴ Thou dost cause the grass to grow for the cattle,
and plants for man to cultivate,
¹⁵ that he may bring forth food from the earth,
and wine to gladden the heart of man,
oil to make his face shine,
and bread to strengthen man's heart.
¹⁶ The trees of the LORD are watered abundantly,
the cedars of Lebanon which he planted.

¹⁷ In them the birds build their nests;
the stork has her home in the fir trees.
¹⁸ The high mountains are for the wild goats;
the rocks are a refuge for the badgers.
¹⁹ Thou hast made the moon to mark the seasons;
the sun knows its time for setting.
²⁰ Thou makest darkness, and it is night,
when all the beasts of the forest creep forth.
²¹ The young lions roar for their prey,
seeking their food from God.
²² When the sun rises, they get them away
and lie down in their dens.
²³ Man goes forth to his work
and to his labor until the evening.

²⁴ O LORD, how manifold are thy works!
In wisdom hast thou made them all;
the earth is full of thy creatures.
²⁵ Yonder is the sea, great and wide,
which teems with things innumerable,
living things both small and great.

26 There go the ships;
   and Leviathan which thou didst form to sport in it.

27 These all look to thee,
   to give them their food in due season.

28 When thou givest to them, they gather it up;
   when thou openest thy hand,
   they are filled with good things.

29 When thou hidest thy face, they are dismayed;
   when thou takest away their breath, they die
   and return to their dust.

30 When thou sendest forth thy Spirit,^s they are created;
   and thou renewest the face of the ground.

31 May the glory of the LORD endure for ever,
   may the LORD rejoice in his works,

32 who looks on the earth and it trembles,
   who touches the mountains and they smoke!

33 I will sing to the LORD as long as I live;
   I will sing praise to my God while I have being.

34 May my meditation be pleasing to him,
   for I rejoice in the LORD.

35 Let sinners be consumed from the earth,
   and let the wicked be no more!
   Bless the LORD, O my soul!
   Praise the LORD!

There is a famous passage in George Borrow's *Lavengro* in which Borrow, unhappy and discontented, is talking to the gipsy Jasper Petulengro. 'Life is sweet, brother,' said Petulengro. 'Do you think so?' asked Borrow. 'Think so!' the gipsy replied. 'There's night and day, brother, both sweet things; sun, moon and stars, brother, all sweet things; there is likewise a wind on the heath. Life is very sweet, brother; who would wish to die?'

'In sickness, Jasper?' asked Borrow. 'There's the sun and the stars,' Jasper answered. 'In blindness, Jasper?' asked Borrow. 'There's the wind on the heath, brother,' answered Jasper. 'If I could only feel that, I would gladly live for ever.'

The world was that way for the poet who wrote this Psalm. It is, says Weiser, 'one of the most beautiful Psalms in the Psalter'. Another commentator says that the Psalmist lived in 'a universe aglow with God'. It has been said that this Psalmist is 'the Wordsworth of the ancients, penetrated with a love for Nature, and gifted with the insight that springs from love'. The Psalm is, as it were, wrapped up in an envelope of praise. It begins: 'Bless the Lord, O my soul! Hallelujah!'

Verses 1-4   THE GREATNESS OF GOD

Bless the Lord, O my soul!
  O Lord my God, thou art very great!
Thou art clothed with honor and majesty,
  who coverest thyself with light as with a garment,
who hast stretched out the heavens like a tent,
  who hast laid the beams of thy chambers on the waters,
who makest the clouds thy chariot,
  who ridest on the wings of the wind,
who makest the winds thy messengers,
  fire and flame thy ministers.

'Thou art very great' – it is the sheer greatness of God which leaves the Psalmist in wondering adoration. Honor and majesty are the garments of royalty.

> The Lord reigns; he is robed in majesty
>
> (Psalm 93.1)

Honor and majesty are before him;
strength and beauty are in his sanctuary

(Psalm 96.6)

It is said of the king:
Splendor and majesty thou dost bestow upon him

(Psalm 21.5)

God covers himself with light as with a garment. There is nothing more natural than the connection of God with the blinding purity of light. 'God is light and in him is no darkness at all' (I John1.5). 'He swells in unapproachable light; and no man has ever seen him or ever can see him' (I Timothy 6.16). Light reveals the truth, and light reveals the flaws, light shows the way, without light no life or growth is possible.

God has stretched out the heavens like a tent. This is a picture of which the poets of the Bible are fond. God, says Isaiah:

Stretches out the heavens like a curtain,
and spreads them like a tent to dwell in

(Isaiah 40.22)

God is the Lord,

who created the heavens and stretched them out

(Isaiah 42.5)

I am the Lord, who made all things,
who stretched out the heavens alone

(Isaiah 44.24)

I made the earth,
and created man upon it;
it was my hands that stretched out the heavens,
and I commanded all their host

(Isaiah 45.12)

God

>stretched out the heavens,
>and laid the foundations of the earth

>(Isaiah 51.13)

>It is he who made the earth by his power,
>>who established the world by his wisdom,
>>and by his understanding stretched out the heavens

>(Jeremiah 10.12)

Two pictures have been seen here. W. E. Barnes sees the picture of God providing the sky like a curtain so that men may not be blinded by the blaze of his glory. 'Clouds and thick darkness are round about him' (Psalm 97.2). Much more likely is the reference to the firmament, the great dome or vault which covered the earth and above which were the upper waters and the abode of God (Genesis 1.6-8). What the Psalmist is saying is that God made the immense dome of the firmament and put it in its place as easily as a man pitches his tent.

God lays the beams of his chambers on the waters. The waters are those waters which are above the dome of the firmament, the waters of the upper world, God's world (Genesis 1.7). The Psalmist says:

>The voice of the Lord is upon the waters;
>>the God of glory thunders,
>>the Lord, upon many waters

>(Psalm 29.3)

>Praise him, you highest heavens,
>and you waters above the heavens!

>(Psalm 148.4)

The word used for the *chambers* of God is that which is used for an upper room. The Palestinian house was flat-roofed like a box and commonly consisted of one room; if a second room was built it was built on a corner of the roof, like a small box on top of a big box, and the upper room was used for rest and prayer and meditation. Amos speaks of God

who builds his upper chambers in the heavens

(Amos 9.6)

So we have the very human picture of God building himself an upper room with beams laid on the waters above the firmament as its foundations. The poet is not thinking as a theologian would think; still less is he thinking as a scientist would; it is a child's picture of heaven, and heaven is very like earth, even to the human touch that God has his own quiet room.

The storm clouds are God's chariots, and the wind is his winged horse.

He came swiftly on the wings of the wind

(Psalm 18.10)

Behold the Lord is riding on a swift cloud

(Isaiah 19.1)

In Daniel the one like a son of man comes riding on the clouds of heaven (Daniel 7.13). At the end time the Son of Man will come riding on the clouds of heaven with power and great glory (Matthew 24.30). It is the picture of God using the elemental forces for his purposes.

God makes the winds his messengers, and fire and flame his servants. The older translations are different; they reverse it and say that God makes his messengers winds and his servants flames of fire. This would mean that when God wished to send a messenger, he, as it were, turned that messenger into a blast of wind or a stroke of lightning. The first way is much more likely; it means that God makes the wind do his bidding and makes the lightning his servant.

There is vividness here and there is poetry; and to take all these pictures with unimaginative literalness is to ruin them. The storm clouds are the chariots of God, the winds are the winged horses of God, the storm blast is his messenger and the flash of lightning his servant. What the Psalmist is saying is that it is his conviction that the whole universe exists to serve the purposes of God; God is the Creator and the Master of all things.

Verses 5-13   CHAOS INTO COSMOS

Thou didst set the earth on its foundations,
   so that it should never be shaken.
Thou didst cover it with the deep as with a garment;
   the waters stood above the mountains.
At thy rebuke they fled;
   at the sound of thy thunder they took to flight.
The mountains rose, the valleys sank down
   to the place which thou didst appoint for them.
Thou didst set a bound which they should not pass,
   so that they might not again cover the earth.

Thou makest springs gush forth in the valleys;
   they flow between the hills,
they give drink to every beast of the field;
   the wild asses quench their thirst.
By them the birds of the air have their habitation;
   they sing among the branches.
From thy lofty abode thou waterest the mountains;
   the earth is satisfied with the fruit of thy work.

The Psalmist is following the order of events in the story of the creation of the world in Genesis 1; and now he comes to the waters. Modern theology believes in creation out of nothing but that was too difficult an idea for the ancient thinkers. They found it impossible – and it is impossible – to conceive of the idea of nothingness. The beginning was a kind of watery chaos. The Genesis story begins: 'The earth was without form and void, and darkness was upon the face of the deep; and the Spirit of God was moving over the face of the waters' (Genesis 1.2).

The basic plan of creation was this. The waters were separated into the waters above and the waters below. They were separated by the firmament, a great overarching vault or dome, held up by pillars. Job, speaking of the action of God, says: 'The pillars of heaven tremble' (Job 26.11). The earth was also supported on pillars and stood on the abyss of the waters under the earth.

Creation of the earth itself begins with the separation of the waters. The waters under the earth are separated from the waters above the earth, above the firmament. The waters are given their place and they cannot move from it. 'By my rebuke I dry up the sea' (Isaiah 50.2). When God was bombarding Job with the statements of his greatness he said:

> Who shut in the sea with doors,
>> when it burst forth from the womb;
> when I made clouds its garment,
>> and thick darkness its swaddling band,
> and prescribed bounds for it,
>> and set bars and doors,
> and said, Thus far you shall come, and no further,
>> and here shall your proud waves be stayed?
>
> (Job 38.8-11)

Proverbs tells how Wisdom was with God at the time of the creation,

> When he assigned to the sea its limit,
>> so that the waters might not transgress his command
>
> (Proverbs 8.29)

Jeremiah hears God say:

> I placed the sand as the bound for the sea,
>> a perpetual barrier which it cannot pass;
> though the waves toss they cannot prevail,
>> though they roar they cannot pass over it
>
> (Jeremiah 5.22)

The very first step in the emergence of the earth was the control of the waters. In the narrative of the Psalmist there is still an echo of a very old myth:

> At thy rebuke they fled;
>> at the sound of thy thunder they took to flight.

The Babylonian story of creation is much more dramatic. In the beginning there was Marduk, the greatest of the gods, the god of order and creation, and there was Tiamat, the goddess of the elemental chaos which was there before the beginning. The Hebrew for the *deep* is *tehom*, which is basically the same word as Tiamat. So creation began with a battle, the battle between Marduk and Tiamat, the battle between the new order and the primeval chaos. Marduk won, and he took Tiamat and split her body in two 'like a flat fish', and he used one half to make the firmament and one half to make the earth. In the Hebrew story God acts solely by the word of his command, but there are still echoes of the old story.

In the story of our Psalmist, even after the waters had been separated, even the mountains were still covered by them. So God routs them by his thunderous word and sends them to their own place. Verse 8 should read as the NEB has it: 'Flowing over the hills, pouring down into the valleys.' So these waters irrigate the hills and the valleys and give drink to the birds and the beasts. Here is the great thought that the waters which were once a part of the threatening chaos have been brought under the control of God to serve his gracious purposes. God has taken what was destructive and made it beneficent.

The last verse of the section, verse 13, has two possible meanings:

> From thy lofty abode thou waterest the mountains;
>   the earth is satisfied with the fruit of thy work.

'The fruit of thy work' can be either the rain which God sends from the heavens, or it can mean that men are satisfied with the fruits of the earth which the gracious action of God gives them.

So the Psalmist's lyric of creation presents us with a picture of a God who brings order out of chaos and who can turn destructive forces into instruments of his mercy.

Verses 14-23   GOD'S CARE FOR MAN AND BEAST

> *Thou dost cause the grass to grow for the cattle,*
>   *and plants for man to cultivate,*
> *that he may bring forth food from the earth,*
>   *and wine to gladden the heart of man,*
> *oil to make his face shine,*
>   *and bread to strengthen man's heart.*
> *The trees of the Lord are watered abundantly,*
>   *the cedars of Lebanon which he planted.*
>
> *In them the birds build their nests;*
>   *the stork has her home in the fir trees.*
> *The high mountains are for the wild goats;*
>   *the rocks are a refuge for the badgers.*
> *Thou hast made the moon to mark the seasons;*
>   *the sun knows its time for setting.*
> *Thou makest darkness, and it is night,*
>   *when all the beasts of the forest creep forth.*

The young lions roar for their prey,
  seeking their food from God.
When the sun rises, they get them away
  and lie down in their dens.
Man goes forth to his work
  and to his labor until the evening.

Again and again the Psalmist tells how the earth is watered by God. In modern society we turn a tap and the water flows; in the northern hemisphere rain is abundant; but in the East water is 'the prime necessity and the great gift'. We would do well not to take for granted the gifts of God which come to us so regularly that we forget that they are gifts. Moses in Deuteronomy reminds the people: 'The Lord your God is bringing you into a good land, a land of brooks of water, of fountains and springs, flowing forth in valleys and hills' (Deuteronomy 8.7).

The second line of verse 14 – 'and plants for man to cultivate' – should more correctly be as in the RSV margin, 'fodder for the animals that serve man', or, as the NEB has it, 'green things for those who toil for man'. God sends food for man and beast.

The three basic products of the land of Palestine were the corn, wine and oil. These were the things of which people were not to forget to give the tithe to God (Deuteronomy 12.17).

Corn gave them their food. *Oil* had many uses. It was used for the protection of the skin. Among the things for which the Psalmist thanks God is that God 'has poured over me fresh oil' (Psalm 92.10). It was used medically for healing. The Samaritan poured wine and oil on the wounds of the stricken traveler (Luke 10.34). It was a regular part of what was called the cereal offering – wine and fine flour and oil (Leviticus 2.4). It was used for anointing. God says of David: 'With my holy oil I have anointed him' (Psalm 89.20). It was used as a sign of gladness. 'Oil and perfume make the heart glad' (Proverbs 27.9). It was used in lamps. In the parable the girls had no oil for their lamps when the bridegroom came (Matthew 25.1-13). It was used for cooking; cakes were baked with oil (Numbers 11.8).

Wine was very commonly drunk, because the water supply was bad; but there was little drunkenness, for the wine was drunk in the proportion of two parts of wine to five of water. Judges speaks of 'wine which cheers gods and men' (Judges 9.13). The Preacher wrote:

> Bread is made for laughter,
>   and wine gladdens life,
>   and money answers everything
>
> (Ecclesiastes 10.19)

Ecclesiasticus writes with typical sages' wisdom:

> Wine and music gladden the heart,
>   but the love of wisdom is better than both
>
> (Ecclesiasticus 40.20)

In verse 19 it is interesting to note that the moon comes first. It was by the moon that the great festivals were dated. 'From the moon comes the sign for feast days,' Ecclesiasticus says (43.7). Oesterley writes: 'Among the Semites at the nomad stage flocks and herds were led to fresh pasturage at night on account of the heat of the day.' It was therefore natural that the moon and not the sun was their chief deity.

Verse 20 brings to our notice what is to us a strange thing about Hebrew thought – 'Thou makest darkness.' Strangely, darkness is a separate, created thing. In the Genesis story there was light and darkness *before* there was sun and moon (Genesis 1.3, 14-19). Darkness is not simply, to the Hebrew mind, an absence of light. It has a separate existence and is related to the

primeval chaos, which God conquered. One of God's questions
fired at Job is:

> Where is the way to the dwelling of light,
> and where is the place of darkness?

(Job 38.19)

From this passage certain great truths emerge.

i. In this world there is nothing that is useless. The mountain
tops may hardly ever be trodden by the feet of men; the rocky
crags may be inaccessible to human beings; but these are the
places where the mountain goats and the badgers have their
homes. Every part of the world is of use for some of God's
creatures.

ii. One of the features of this Psalm is its interest in the
beasts – the beasts of the field, the wild asses, the cattle, the
birds, the stork, the wild goats, the badgers. Even the roar of the
young lions at night is regarded as a kind of prayer to God for
their food. As W. E. Barnes puts it, the world was not made
simply for the profit of human beings. God feeds the young
lions as well as the children of men. All that lives belongs to God
and is dear to him. As Coleridge made the Ancient Mariner say
to the Wedding Guest:

> Farewell, farewell! but this I tell
> To thee, thou Wedding Guest!
> He prayeth well who loveth well
> Both man and bird and beast.
>
> He prayeth best who loveth best
> All things both great and small,
> For the dear God who loveth us,
> He made and loveth all.

iii. God gives men not simply the things which support life, but also the things which enable a man to enjoy life, not simply the corn and the food, but the oil as a sign of gladness and the wine which makes glad the heart of man. God did not mean a man simply to have life; he meant him also to enjoy it.

Verses 24-35   MERCY AND MIGHT

O Lord, how manifold are thy works!
  In wisdom hast thou made them all;
  the earth is full of thy creatures.
Yonder is the sea, great and wide,
  which teems with things innumerable,
  living things both small and great.
There go the ships,
  and Leviathan which thou didst form to sport in it.

These all look to thee,
  to give them their food in due season.
When thou givest to them, they gather it up;
  when thou openest thy hand,
  they are filled with good things.
When thou hidest thy face, they are dismayed;
  when thou takest away their breath, they die
  and return to their dust.
When thou sendest forth thy Spirit, they are created;
  and thou renewest the face of the ground.

May the glory of the Lord endure for ever,
  may the Lord rejoice in his works,
who looks on the earth and it trembles,
  who touches the mountains and they smoke!
I will sing to the Lord as long as I live;
  I will sing praise to my God while I have being.

> *May my meditation be pleasing to him,*
> > *for I rejoice in the Lord.*
> *Let sinners be consumed from the earth,*
> > *and let the wicked be no more!*
> *Bless the Lord, O my soul!*
> *Praise the Lord!*

Now the eyes and the thoughts of the Psalmist turn to the sea. To the Hebrew the sea was always awe-inspiring and mysterious.

> Three things are too wonderful for me;
> > four I do not understand;
> the way of an eagle in the sky,
> > the way of a serpent on a rock,
> the way of a ship on the high seas,
> > and the way of a man with a maiden
>
> > (Proverbs 30.18, 19)

Even more to the Hebrew the sea was terrifying. In the vision of the time to be John of the Revelation sees a world in which 'the sea was no more' (Revelation 21.1). But even the mysterious and terrifying sea is filled with creatures God has made. On the sea are the ships; in the sea is the largest of all God's creatures – the immense Leviathan, sea monster or sea serpent or whale. There are two ways of taking the second half of verse 26. It may be taken as the RSV takes it – 'Leviathan which thou didst form to sport in it'. As one commentator has put it: 'The sea is the playground of the mighty ones.' But both the NEB and the Jerusalem Bible take it differently. The NEB has, 'Leviathan whom thou hast made thy plaything', and the Jerusalem Bible has even more vividly, 'Leviathan whom you made to amuse you'. God in his barrage of questions to Job says of Leviathan: 'Will you play with him as with a bird?'; and the implication is that, though Job cannot, God can (Job 41.5). And so the thought of the Psalmist most likely is that the largest and the strangest and the wildest creatures are the tame pets and playthings of God.

In verses 27-30 the Psalmist remembers that all living creatures are utterly dependent on God.

> The eyes of all look to thee,
>> and thou givest them their food in due season.
> Thou openest thy hand,
>> thou satisfiest the desire of every living thing
>
>> (Psalm 145.15, 16)
>
> He gives to the beasts their food,
> and to the young ravens which cry
>
>> (Psalm 147.9)

As Jane Taylor's old hymn has it:

> 'Tis thou preservest me from death
>> And dangers every hour;
> I cannot draw another breath
>> Unless thou give me power.

All living creatures are dependent on God for the food they eat and for the breath they breathe. The Hebrew word *ruach* means breath and spirit and wind. The old creation story tells how God formed man from the dust of the ground, and then 'breathed into his nostrils the breath of life; and man became a living being' (Genesis 2.7). And at the end of life, as the Preacher says: 'The dust returns to the earth as it was, and the spirit returns to God who gave it' (Ecclesiastes 12.7). All is of God. And because of that the Psalmist can see life as a continuing and continuous creation. 'When thou sendest forth thy spirit they are created.' Each new living creature is to the Psalmist a new creation of God.

But the thought of the mercy of God must not obliterate the memory of his might. The earth trembling with the earthquake and the mountain smoking with the volcano are also the work of God.

> His lightnings lighten the world;
>> the earth sees and trembles.
> The mountains melt like wax before the Lord,
>> before the Lord of all the earth

(Psalm 97.4, 5)

> Bow thy heavens, O Lord, and come down!
>> Touch the mountains that they smoke!

(Psalm 144.5)

It is the Lord God of Hosts

> who touches the earth and it melts

(Amos 9.5)

So in view of the might of God the Psalmist concludes with two thoughts. First, he realizes again the duty of praising God's mercy and God's might and of meditating on them, and he prays that his praise and his meditation may form an acceptable sacrifice to God. Second, if the true harmony of creation is to be achieved, then, as he puts it, sinners must be consumed from the earth.

The prayer for the destruction of sinners has in it what looks like savagery which offends modern ears. But three things have to be noted. First the Hebrew thought very concretely. We would pray for the destruction of *sin*; the Hebrew personalized it and prayed for the destruction of the *sinner*. And he was thinking far more of destruction of sin than of the destruction of particular people. Second, there is nothing personal in this.

The central fact in Israel's life was the covenant, the special relationship between God and Israel, and that covenant depended on Israel keeping the law of God. So the Psalmist was thinking more of the protection of the covenant than the destruction of the sinner. Third, and it is another way to say the same thing, the Psalmist was moved not by hatred of the sinner, but by his supreme desire to see God, the Creator and Lord of the world, acknowledged and revered as such. True, the Psalmist has not yet reached the stage when it can be said that he hates the sin but loves the sinner, but he is at the stage when he is moved not so much by hatred of the sinner as by love of God.

THE FEARLESS THINKER

When we were studying Psalm 19, we noted that when a man has a completely unshakable faith in the true God, he has no hesitation in using pictures and thoughts, no matter whence they come. The writer of Psalm 104 had the same fearless open-mindedness.

There are two Egyptian hymns which show remarkable parallels to the thought of this Psalm. The first is called 'The Praise of Amon-Re'. Amon-Re was at that time the greatest of the Egyptian gods; the date of the hymn is 1450 BC. Here is how certain parts of it run:

> Thou, the Only One, who didst create what is . . . Thou out of whose eyes men proceeded, and out of whose mouth the gods arose. Who didst create herbage for the herds, and the fruit tree for men. Who didst make that whereon the fishes in the streams live, and the birds . . . Who givest breath to that which is in the egg, and dost nourish the little worm. Who providest that whereon the gnats live. Who providest that whereof the mice in their holes have need . . . Hail to thee who didst create all this,

thou Only One with the many arms (the arms are the rays of the sun). Who while men sleep, dost watch and bring night to an end, and seekest that which is best for his flock, as a good shepherd.

There is the same thought of God's detailed care for all his creatures as we find in the Psalm. The second is the great hymn of Pharaoh Amen-hotep the Fourth, Ikhnaton, to the Sun; it is the hymn to Aton, the rays of the Sun, and Ikhnaton reigned in Egypt from 1375 to 1358 BC:

> Thou appearest in beauty on the horizons of heaven,
> Thou living sun, the first to live,
> Thou risest on the eastern horizon,
> Suffusing all lands with thy beauty.
> Glorious art thou, and mighty,
> Shining on high o'er the lands.
> Thy rays encircle the countries
> To the farthest limit of all thy creation;
> Thou art Re (the Sun-god) reaching out to their uttermost
> border,
> Subduing them for thy beloved son (the son is Pharaoh).
> Far off art thou, yet thy beams touch the earth;
> Thou art seen of men, but thy pathway they know not.
>
> Thou settest in the western horizon,
> And the earth becometh dark as death.
> Men rest in their chambers,
> With head enveloped, no eye sees aught;
> Should their goods be taken that lie under their heads,
> They would fail to perceive it.
> The lion comes forth from his lair,
> And the serpents bite.
> Darkness rules, and the earth is still,
> For he that made all resteth in the horizon.

When the earth becometh light, thou risest on the horizon,
And, as the sun, dost illumine the day;
The darkness fleeth, when thy rays thou dost spread;
The two lands (Upper and Lower Egypt) rejoice;
They awake, stand up on their feet,
When thou hast raised them up;
They cleanse their bodies and clothe themselves,
Their arms give praise (by being lifted up), for thou hast
    appeared.
The whole earth goeth forth to labor,
The cattle are satisfied with grass;
The trees and the herbs grow green,
The birds from their nests fly forth,
With their wings they offer thee praise.
The beasts spring up on their feet,
The birds and every flying thing
Live, when thou art risen.

So once again we see that the Psalmist is so sure of his own faith that he can take and appropriate beauty wherever he may find it. As Weiser put it of the writer of Psalm 19: 'Faith liberates him from any fearful timidity . . . He has an ear for man's elemental response . . . to the impressive language of Nature which is understood by every sensitive human being, including the Gentiles.' The Psalmist, says Oesterley, 'utilizes and adapts the conceptions and beliefs of people who do not acknowledge Jahweh as their God . . . He discerns some element of truth in the ancient conception.' He sees 'crude germs of truth seized on by men struggling towards the light through darkness, granted by the self-revealing God'. Here also, then, is the truth that fifteen hundred years before Jesus came into the world men were stretching upwards and were catching however distantly some glimpse of God.

In this Psalm there are three great truths about the world in which we live.

i. The Psalm lays down what our attitude to the world should be. In the Mishnah there is a tractate entitled Berakoth, which means blessings; it lays down the blessings a man should say when he sees certain things. 'If a man saw shooting stars, earthquakes, lightnings, thunders and storms, he should say, Blessed is he whose power and might fill the world. If he saw mountains, hills, seas, rivers and deserts, he should say, Blessed is the author of creation . . . For rain and good tidings he should say, Blessed is he the Good and the Doer of Good. For bad tidings he should say, Blessed is he the true Judge.' It was the Jewish view that for everything in the world there was a blessing. In the Jewish Prayer Book a man is taught to say, Blessed art thou, O Lord our God, when he sees the ocean or a high mountain, and when he first sees trees blossoming in spring. There is an unwritten saying of Jesus, one of those that were passed down by word of mouth but which never got into the written Gospels: 'He that wonders shall reign, and he that reigns shall find rest.' The Jew never ceased to wonder at the world – and the Christian must be the same.

ii. This Psalm shows us the character of the world. In the world two things are wonderfully combined – purpose and beauty. Things can be useful and yet lack all grace and attractiveness and charm; they can be bleakly utilitarian. Things can be beautiful but useless; they can belong to the luxuries rather than to the necessities of life. In God's creation usefulness and beauty go hand in hand. And God's method in creation should be man's aim in his workmanship.

iii. This Psalm tells us something about the relationship of the Creator to his world. There are two adjectives which are used of God. He is said to be transcendent. To call God transcendent is to say that he is outside and above the world, that in might and majesty and power he is far distant from all ordinary things. God is said to be immanent. To call him immanent is to say that he is involved in the world and is part of the world. This Psalm most wonderfully combines the transcendence and the immanence of God. It never loses sight of the sheer majesty and holiness of God, and at the same time never loses the conviction that God is in the world which he has made.